telephoto photography
by kalton c. lahue

telephoto

PETERSEN'S PHOTO PUBLISHING GROUP

PHOTO SPECIALTY PUBLICATIONS
Paul R. Farber/Editorial Director
Mike Stensvold/Editor
Gary M Schuster/Art Director
Charlene Marmer Solomon/Editorial Assistant
Laurie Wright/Assistant Art Director

PHOTOGRAPHIC MAGAZINE
Paul R. Farber/Editor and Publisher
Karen Sue Geller/Managing Editor
Jim Creason/Art Director
Joan Yarfitz/Feature Editor
Markene Kruse-Smith/Movie Editor
David B. Brooks/Technical Editor
Steven I. Rosenbaum/East Coast Editor
Elissa Rabellino/Associate Editor
Bill Hurter/Editorial Assistant
Wanda Acevedo/Vazquez/Assistant Art Director
Natalie Carroll/Administrative Assistant
Ed Becker/Contributing Editor
Ben Helprin/Contributing Editor
Kalton C. Lahue/Contributing Editor
Steve Poster/Contributing Editor
Robert D. Routh/Contributing Editor
David Sutton/Contributing Editor
Parry C. Yob/Contributing Editor

PETERSEN PUBLISHING COMPANY
R. E. Petersen/Chairman of the Board
F. R. Waingrow/President
Herb Metcalf/Senior Vice President
Philip E. Trimbach/Vice President, Finance
William Porter/Vice President, Circulation Director
Jack Thompson/Circulation Assistant Director
Nigel P. Heaton/Circulation Marketing Director
T. Swift Lockard/Advertising Marketing Director
Arthur Zarin/Research Director
Spencer Nilson/Administrative Services Director
Alan C. Hahn/Market Development Director
James J. Krenek/Manufacturing Services Director
Al Isaacs/Graphics Director
Bob D'Olivo/Photography Director
Maria Cox/Data Processing Services Manager

TELEPHOTO PHOTOGRAPHY
By Kalton C. Lahue. Copyright © 1977 by Petersen Publishing Co., 8490 Sunset Blvd., Los Angeles, Calif. 90069. Phone (213) 657-5100. All rights reserved. No part of this book may be reproduced without written permission from the publisher. Printed in U.S.A.

Library of Congress Catalog Card Number/77-074103
ISBN/0-8227-4021-4

COVER
Front cover: Transparency sandwich taken by Mike Sheras. The boat was shot with a 200mm Zuiko using Kodachrome 64 film, and the sun was taken with 600mm Vivitar Solid Cat and 2X converter with Ektachrome 200. Inside front cover photo by Glenn Cooper with 135mm lens. Inside back cover photo by John Guarente with 70-210 Vivitar zoom lens. Photo on this page by Hal Stoelzle taken with a 135mm lens. Cover design by Gary M Schuster.

4 the telephoto mystique

8 handling the telephoto lens

18 85-105mm

22 120-150mm

26 180-300mm

30 350-600mm

34 800-2000mm

38 telephoto color gallery

46 telephoto zooms

50 close-focusing zooms

54 catadioptric lenses

58 press and view camera telephotos

60 auxiliary telephoto devices

62 tele-converters

70 macro-focusing telephotos

76 tripods

the telephoto mystique

As most photographers are aware, the telephoto or long focus lens is one whose focal length has been expressly designed to cover a smaller or narrower angular field of view on a given film format than the one considered as "normal" for that particular format—in other words, it "sees" less, while bringing distant objects much closer to the camera. For 35mm fans, any focal length greater than 50-58mm is considered a telephoto; for the 6x6 user, focal lengths greater than 75-85mm are considered telephotos, etc.

Telephoto lenses have always held a considerable fascination for amateur photographers—no one denies that they're always handy for peering through your neighbor's window to see "what's going on," and you'd probably be surprised to learn how many purchasers actually count this among their justifications for the purchase of a 400mm "girl watcher" special. Every time something spectacular happens involving the use of a telephoto lens, such as the photos taken at the 1975 Helsinki Conference of Henry Kissinger perusing top-secret documents in which the contents were clearly revealed to the camera, the "spy syndrome" sets off another healthy rash of telephoto sales in the amateur market. And why not? Photographer Franco Rossi cashed in to the tune of $17,000+ in picture sales for that series.

While the ultimate in focal lengths and lens speeds have already been attained commensurate with the optical state of the art, new and refined telephoto designs continue to appear with increasing frequency, offering better optical correction, the use of new, exotic forms of glass to achieve this reduction in aberrations, and less-complicated mechanisms housed in smaller and smaller barrels. But all of these advancements come at a price, and while one end of the focal length range grows increasingly inexpensive, its opposite end grows considerably more costly with each new advance.

Since you chose this particular book from the large selection available in Petersen's How-To Photographic Library, it seems safe to assume that (a) you own a camera whose lens can be interchanged, (b) whether or not you already own one or more interchangeable optics, you're interested in learning more about working with telephoto lenses, and (c) you're somewhat conversant with basic lens/focal length theory. Should you be confused about (c) or the mechanics of selecting/purchasing additional optics for your camera, *Interchangeable Lenses* (another of the Petersen Library) deals with the basics and provides specific advice to help you decide how to best spend your money. This book has been created to assist you in putting a telephoto lens to use creatively.

WHY A TELEPHOTO?

Many amateur photographers are captivated with the potential offered by the telephoto to reach out into space and bring into view a distant object that's otherwise unrecognizable when photographed with the camera's normal lens. The normal lens will deliver an image about the same size as that seen by the naked eye; double that focal length and you double the image size. Unfortunately, too many think of the telephoto mainly in that respect—if you can't get close enough, use the longer focal length lens—completely overlooking the creative potential such lenses possess. Thus enticed by the prospects of candid pictures taken at great distances, the ability to deal effectively with distant subjects of interest when the camera cannot be brought closer to them, and the revelation of objects, patterns and textures invisible to the naked eye, they will usually acquire a telephoto before considering a wide-angle simply because the effect through the viewfinder is much more pronounced, and so the optics sell themselves with little or no effort on the part of the salesperson. All too frequently, the only question asked is, "How much?" instead of, "Is this really going to be a useful purchase for me?"

Like the wide-angle, the telephoto is a specialized lens, and the farther up the focal length ladder you travel from the accepted norm, the more specialized its use becomes. Certainly, there are times when you simply cannot get the desired picture without the help of a telephoto, but many photographers have a tendency to prefer its use for a reason that's psychologically insidious—they're afraid to become involved with their subject. It's one thing to snap a head-and-shoulder candid of that cute blonde from across the street, but quite another to approach the little lady with a 35mm lens and interact with a total stranger in such a way as to get the desired shot.

1. Do the Blue Angels really fly this close? Well, they're good, but to do this they had a little help from the 1250mm Celestron used by W.J. Beecher. Such compression effects of long focal length lenses scream telephoto, but are still breathtaking. (Courtesy of Celestron International and W. J. Beecher.) 2. The 135mm is considered a good lens for portraits, as it allows the photographer to work at a distance sufficient to avoid any facial distortion of his subject. (Ron Berkenblitt.)

Because of its ability to reach across great distances, the telephoto lends itself to a more detached subject viewpoint, and while it's possible to achieve as effective a photograph with a wide-angle lens on many occasions, the two extremes in focal lengths produce different statements about how you feel relative to your subject. Of course, if you're photographing a building, a scenic, a sports activity, etc., the telephoto may well be a necessity, but you shouldn't allow the focal length to determine your approach to a subject.

In other words, it's all too easy to rely upon a telephoto as a crutch instead of letting your subject determine your approach, and thus the focal length to be used. If you fall into the all-too-common trap of letting your lens dictate how you'll treat a particular subject, you'll quickly exhaust the creative potential of whatever telephotos you have, and they'll gather dust in your gadget bag.

Thus to answer our question of why a telephoto, it should be for growth on your part as a photographer. Granted that every new lens you acquire has an initial fascination all its own, but you must have both the desire and the willingness to explore the potential of the lens beyond that point if it is to become a useful tool in expanding your photographic horizons. To that end, the following chapters are devoted and should provide sufficient food for thought to help you see beyond the lure and siren call of the telephoto lens.

WHICH TELEPHOTO?

While selecting a suitable telephoto lens is more difficult than choosing the most appropriate wide-angle lens, cost alone will hold many readers to the 400mm as a maximum focal length. And unlike most wide-angles, which can be put to a wide variety of uses despite their short focal lengths and great coverage, the extreme telephotos with their much reduced angular field of view

(two degrees to five degrees) tend to have a restricted value to the average photographer.

For all practical purposes then, your selection will be made from a telephoto range available in 85, 100, 105, 135, 180, 200, 250, 300 and 400mm focal lengths (not all of which are available for the same camera) with diagonal angles of view of 29, 24, 23, 18, 14, 12, 10, eight and six degrees, in that order. Unlike wide-angle lenses, whose maximum aperture can often be held to f/2.8 or f/4 well down the focal length range, the longer telephotos are usually much slower in speed (f/8 or f/11) and the mechanical complexities involved make an automatic diaphragm rare on most optics longer than 400mm. Not surprisingly, the price of a telephoto lens (beyond the moderate focal length range) generally increases as its focal length increases, and those beyond 800mm are often out of reach of the amateur who will rarely find sufficient use for one to justify its purchase. But there are ways around this particular problem for those on a restricted budget, as we'll see in later chapters.

Wherever you turn, you'll probably be told that a moderate telephoto (85-135mm) is your best bet as a first acquisition, and I'm in full agreement with this advice for many reasons. The initial impact as seen through the viewfinder may not be as startling as that of a 400mm, but neither are the negative factors which come into play as your focal length increases. The moderate telephoto is hand-holdable and will not require much deviation from your accepted photographic procedure, beyond the use of a somewhat higher shutter speed than you may be accustomed to as a means of preventing camera movement. And with the latest trend in lens design, which we'll discuss at length in the next chapter, the size and weight of many such telephotos is shrinking rapidly to a point where they're not any more difficult to handle than the camera's standard lens.

1. When used properly, telephoto shots need not reveal their focal length. This aerial stunt was captured from the ground by Ron Berkenblitt using a 400mm.
2. A favorite of sports photographers, the 200mm took Glenn Cooper from the sidelines right into the middle of the action as Terry Bradshaw prepared to run in this Rams vs. Steelers contest.
3. The long telephoto is a necessity when photographing subjects like surfers. This 600mm shot from the shoreline put Ron Berkenblitt right out where the action is.
4. Camera trickery combined with a 400mm telephoto to produce this ghostlike double image of a cycle racer. Ron Berkenblitt held in the rewind button for a motor-driven double exposure. Shots like this require distance between camera and subject for safety, and it's the telephoto that makes the difference.

In order to develop a strong feeling for both the lens and what it will do, I recommend that you mount the telephoto to your camera body and take several picture expeditions equipped with only that lens. In this way, you'll force yourself to rethink many picture opportunities, and the resulting self-discipline developed in this manner will become an invaluable tool that you could probably not acquire in any other manner. And once you've become accustomed to "seeing" with the telephoto lens, you should be able to look at a potential subject and determine the most effective treatment as well as the focal length required to do the job, just as many photographers can eyeball the correct exposure within one-half f-stop without resorting to the use of a light meter at all.

As you'll see in later chapters, the effects that you can achieve by using a telephoto lens and the pictures which result will not only be considerably different than anything you've done before, but will probably quicken your interest in acquiring more and different lenses. But in order to obtain such results, you'll need a personal commitment to your telephoto and its use, or it'll end up at the bottom of your gadget bag gathering dust.

To get the most from any telephoto lens, you must become completely familiar with its advantages, disadvantages and eccentricities. In addition, the telephoto presents a number of problems peculiar to its greater focal length. To use one most effectively, you must first understand the nature of these problems and how they affect the focal length you have chosen to use, so we'll look into that topic next. □

You'll also find a good deal more use for the moderate telephoto than for one of the more exotic focal lengths, unless your photography is almost exclusively involved with something like football. The moderate telephoto is easier to carry with you, can be purchased with a maximum aperture close to that of your standard lens, and should not break your budget wide open to add one or more to your gadget bag. In many cases, the use of a moderate telephoto will allow you to crop your subject in the camera instead of in the darkroom, producing a better quality image which will result in a superior print.

During the past few years, the moderate zoom lens has also become more popular as its image-producing quality has increased and its price decreased. While the decision of whether to buy a prime single focal length telephoto or a zoom lens will ultimately rest with the user, you should very carefully consider the pros and cons of each before you purchase. While a zoom is convenient, it is also bulky, somewhat heavier and generally slower in maximum speed, yet the compositional assistance afforded by the ability to pick a given focal length right to a silly millimeter should not be overlooked. But for those new to the interchangeable lens game, I would still recommend a single focal length telephoto, as the zoom has a tendency to make an already lazy photographer (which most of us are) still lazier.

WHEN TO USE THE TELEPHOTO?

Regardless of whatever focal length telephoto you may already own or are anxious to buy, carrying it in your gadget bag as a second lens means that it will receive use primarily when you desire to reach out and pull a subject or a portion of one in closer to the camera. While that's one very valid reason for the use of a telephoto, it is by no means the only one you should consider.

handling the telephoto lens

Telephoto lenses have a number of distinct characteristics which make their use and handling considerably different from that of wide-angles. While it's possible to duplicate the telephoto effect by simply enlarging a portion of a negative taken with the camera's normal 50-58mm lens, it's not often practical to rely upon this technique. Not only will the grain structure from the greatly enlarged negative segment give away your technique, but you will not be able to put those characteristics peculiar to long focal length lenses to work for you in a creative manner. The end result will be nothing more or less than a very selectively cropped picture, and telephoto photography should be more than just selective cropping.

THE PHYSICAL LENS

Telephotos bend light rays less than do shorter focal lengths. Because of the greater distance between the optical center of the telephoto lens and the film plane, telephotos are longer than standard lenses. Some are mammoth by comparison, dwarfing the camera body to an extent

that makes it appear to be little more than an appendage to the tube of glass. Focusing and aperture controls are usually quite far apart, so you should have no difficulty in using them, although Soligor's new "One-Touch" design offers a direction in which other manufacturers are sure to follow. The Soligor design relies upon a single ring for both focusing and aperture control—revolve the ring left or right to focus; draw back on the ring until you feel the detent and then turn to change the aperture setting. Arranging the controls in this manner allows the user to keep his eye to the viewfinder while performing either function with absolute accuracy, preventing the possibility of disturbing one setting while fumbling for the other, or removing the eye from the viewfinder to make certain that the hand settles on the right control.

Most telephoto lenses longer than 200mm will have a rotating collar that contains a built-in tripod socket and a thumb screw to securely hold the collar in whatever position the user desires. This is quite necessary and most desirable, as long lenses mounted to any camera body must be adequately supported. If not, the increased weight will place excessive stress on the camera's mounting flange or screw threads. Because of this greater length and weight, hand-holding a camera equipped with most lenses longer than 200mm can prove to be quite troublesome, resulting in camera movement even during the relatively brief moment of exposure. Unless getting the picture is of more importance than its quality, it is best to plan on using most telephoto lenses longer than 135mm with a tripod or some other form of camera support, although there are a few lenses that can be considered as exceptions to this rule, as we'll see.

You'll find that barrel diameters and the sizes of filters required to fit them vary greatly according to the speed, focal length and manufacturer of telephoto lenses, but most designers are currently making a determined effort to keep them within reasonable boundaries, even if they are not able to maintain the use of a single filter size throughout the focal length range they offer. This has its practical aspects in terms of the number of different filters necessary to service all the lenses you might own, while keeping the total cost down to an affordable level. As such, it might well prove a factor of concern to those dedicated filter users.

Retractable lens hoods are appearing on more and more telephotos in place of the screw-in hoods usually furnished. These can be a blessing or a curse, depending upon how well you function with them. While there's no doubt that the retractable feature makes the hood easier to carry along without becoming excess baggage, many of them do not have sufficient frictional contact to hold them in place, whether pulled out for use or retracted for carrying.

Because of the greatly narrowed angle of view, it's important that you use the proper lens hood when working with a telephoto lens. While the hood from your 135mm may well fit the barrel of your 200mm, it was not designed for use with that focal length and will not do the job adequately. Switching hoods and using one from a 200mm with a 135mm lens is quite apt to lead to vignetting, especially at larger apertures. If your telephoto lens does not have a retractable hood, you should pick up the one

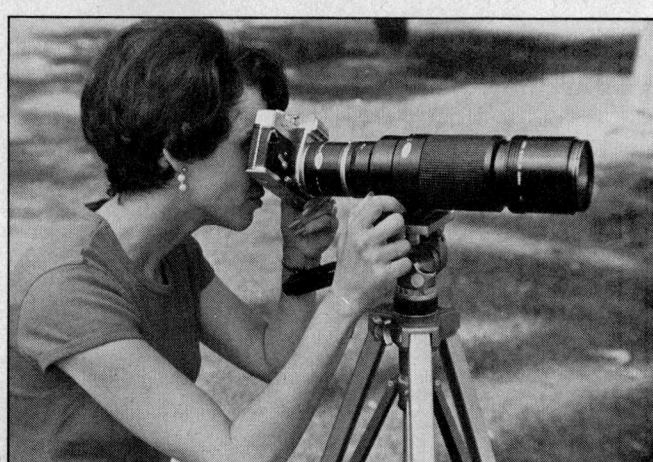

1. The longer the telephoto focal length, the more restricted its use becomes, not only from choice of subject, but in how it's handled.
2. Only a long telephoto has the ability to reach across space. Photographing this arriving ship in the harbor with a normal lens would produce far too small an image. (Jeff Blackwell.)
3. Physical size is one restriction. The 85mm shown here isn't much larger than a normal focal length. For longer focal lengths, manufacturers have chosen different ways to hold size down to manageable proportions. The 500mm mirror lens (center) is one way; a 2X converter matched to a particular lens design is another. This 400mm f/5.6 APO Tele-Rokkor becomes an f/11 800mm with the converter attached.
4. A rotating tripod collar has three distinct advantages with lenses greater than 180-200mm: (1) it takes the strain of the lens's weight off the body, (2) lets you align the camera body perfectly level, or (3) deliberately misalign the body to frame a subject from perfectly horizontal to full vertical without stressing the tripod's camera platform.

specifically designed for the lens, and use it for that focal length only.

Interestingly enough, there's been considerable progress recently in reducing the total size, weight and bulk of the moderate through medium range of telephoto lenses. Since the introduction of the Olympus OM-1 design in 1972, manufacturers have been scrambling to keep up with the trend toward more compact optics. Miranda followed suit with its EC series of lenses and virtually every major camera manufacturer has now taken the hint, with even the tradition-conscious Nikon gradually replacing older optics with improved and redesigned "mini" versions. For example, Nikon has replaced its long-lived 135mm f/2.8 Nikkor with a newer version that's about 20 percent smaller in size and weighs six ounces (30 percent) less than the older lens. The compact trend shows no signs of diminishing in focal lengths to 135mm, and will probably be extended up the focal length ladder as technology permits.

In the medium-to-super telephoto range, such reductions are not as easily attained because of the nature of the beast, but the increasing use of fluorite crystal and fluorocrown glass with their exceptional light-dispersing properties reduces chromatic aberrations in such designs. This provides superior correction, good contrast and crisp definition, and in combination with newer optical formulas, has resulted in some of the most compact long lenses yet seen. Of course, such optics don't come inexpensively, but at this writing, these designs definitely point the way to the future, as does the trend toward the ultracompact designs in the moderate-to-medium focal lengths.

What does this all have to do with handling the telephoto lens? Better corrected optics will deliver better image quality that is not as easily degraded by camera movement (and other factors), and the smaller, lightweight lenses will reduce the possibility of such movement occurring during exposure. Thus, weight, length and barrel diameter will become even more important considerations when selecting a really long focal length lens. In other words, we can look forward in the very near future to an increasing number of telephoto lenses which will be as easy to work with as are present normal focal lengths, and this can only result in far better pictures with far less problems.

In the meantime, should you rush down to your camera shop and trade in your present telephoto lenses for the newer and more compact versions? For most of us, that's a great temptation, but hardly a practical approach. If you have been unable to get really satisfactory pictures with lenses you already own, you probably won't do any better with the newer and smaller versions. The major importance of this trend toward compact design is one of convenience, and simply having a lens that's more convenient to use does not guarantee better pictures. If and when you find it desirable to upgrade your current lenses with faster optics, or when you're looking to fill in a blank in the range of focal lengths you already have, the compact designs offer a sensible alternative to some of the problems in handling telephoto lenses, that's all.

1. Retractable lens hoods mean that you no longer have to fumble in the gadget bag for an accessory you left behind.
2. New telephoto lens designs make use of fluorite crystal and fluorocrown glass; the 600mm f/5.6 ED-Nikkor is one example.
3. Screw-in diopter correction lenses for those whose eyesight is not as good as it once was will make precise focusing with the telephoto easier.

ANGLE OF VIEW

How much will a telephoto lens actually "see?" That depends upon its focal length—the longer the focal length, the less it will "see." This is known as its angle of view (Figure A). The 50mm lens considered as "normal" for a 35mm camera has an angle of view of 46 degrees, computed on the basis of the negative's diagonal (not from side-to-side) and calculated with the lens focused at infinity. Actually, the telephoto will "see" somewhat less than its stated angle of view; that is, the horizontal field of view—what the camera sees from one side of the negative to the other—is not as great as the diagonal.

Thus while a 135mm has a stated angle of view (diagonal) of 18 degrees, the horizontal field of view is really 15 degrees. Many photographers tend to confuse the diagonal with the horizontal, primarily because the two-dimensional diagrams which are used to explain angle of view are presented in a visually misleading manner. For most of us, angle of view is helpful only in selecting another lens to complement those we already own. As long as you understand that you're not really covering a 29-degree angle from side-to-side when you buy an 85mm lens (it's actually 24 degrees), angle-of-view figures can be used for comparative purposes, even though they do not convey a really meaningful difference between focal lengths.

ANGLE OF VIEW—35mm FORMAT

FOCAL LENGTH (MM)	DIAGONAL	HORIZONTAL
50	46°	40°
85	29°	24°
90	27°	22°
100	24°	20°
105	23°	19°
120	20°	17°
135	18°	15°
150	16.5°	14°
180	14°	12°
200	12°	10°
250	9°	8°
300	8°	6°52'
400	6°	5°8'
500	5°	4°
600	4°	3°26'
800	3°	2°34'
1000	2.5°	2°4'

FIGURE A

DEPTH OF FIELD AND FOCUSING

The longer the focal length of a lens, the easier it seems to focus. Revolve the focusing ring only slightly and images will pop into sharp register with absolute certainty. But strangely enough, many photographers have difficulty obtaining really sharp telephoto pictures, even when their camera and lens are mounted on a sturdy tripod—why?

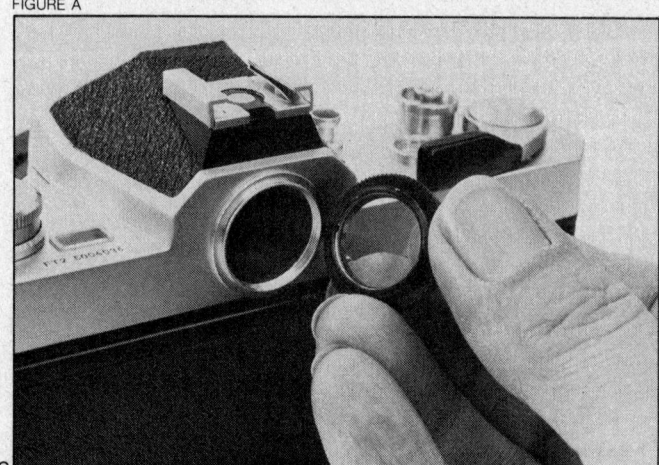

As we'll see, atmospheric interference, chromatic aberration, lowered contrast and camera movement can all play a role in reducing the sharpness of any picture taken with a telephoto lens, but incorrect focusing on the part of the photographer is the most common culprit. While the focusing screens in modern SLR cameras are usually satisfactory when working at full aperture, or under good lighting conditions, the quality of an individual's eyesight plays a larger role than you might suspect.

We're all aware of the focusing difficulties encountered by those who wear eyeglasses. Because of the problems in getting their eye close to and centered behind the eyepiece, they seem to have equal difficulty in using either the microprism or split-image screens with which most 35mm SLRs are equipped. Actually, the full-focusing screen is a far better choice for telephoto work, as it lets you check the sharpness of any part of the subject without requiring that you center a small spot in the middle of the screen on that part of the subject. Yet this type of focusing screen is less than useful for wide-angle or general work, and so the one found in most SLR cameras is usually a compromise. If your camera permits easy interchange of the focusing screens, do so when working with longer focal lengths. Those whose cameras have a fixed pentaprism and focusing screen should work with more care in focusing.

At the same time, there are many photographers who should work with a diopter lens in the viewfinder system to correct minor vision difficulties. These are usually available in a variety of corrections and simply screw into the rear of the viewfinder eyepiece. Unfortunately, they either do not realize that such help is available, or are unaware that they need this assistance in viewing. And so they attempt to focus the camera to accommodate what their slightly faulty eye accepts as being a sharp point of focus, but what actually turns out to be a point of soft focus at the film plane. If you have minor vision problems, the diopter lens can be an answer to focusing difficulties.

Such problems are often

compounded by the focusing method the average photographer uses. Although a telephoto image leaps in and out of focus with ease, the common tendency is to rack the lens beyond its sharpest focus point and back to one that's out of focus, repeating this exercise in shorter passes until the user feels that he's right on the mark. Unfortunately, this is not only time-consuming when working with many subjects, but it's also visually confusing, often to the point that you'll find it very difficult to judge the *exact* point of greatest sharpness. A far better method is to simply rack the lens one time only, stopping on the way back at what appears to be the sharpest point of focus—more often than not, you'll be right where you should be.

Remember, depth of field at a given aperture decreases as the focal length increases. In many cases, missing the desired plane of focus by a mere fraction can accentuate your focusing error sufficiently to make the end result unacceptable when the negative is blown up or the slide projected. The importance of accurate focusing can be seen by looking at a typical moderate telephoto design—a 135mm f/3.5 with a minimum focusing distance of five feet. When used at its maximum aperture and focused on an object five feet from the camera, the sharpness range is but a mere 1¼ inches; when the lens is focused on an object 30 feet away, the range of acceptable sharpness extends only 3⅓ feet from the front to the rear of the point of focus.

A look at Figure B is even more enlightening in making this point. Using each of the stated lenses at its maximum aperture and focusing on an object 50 feet from the camera will give a decreasing depth-of-field

1-2. *The limited depth of field with long telephotos requires critical focusing, even at apertures of f/11 and smaller. In (1), the 800mm lens was focused on the railing, throwing the trees just a few feet behind it out of focus. As the trees are brought into semisharp focus with a slight turn of the focusing ring (2), the foreground subjects go almost completely out of focus. You'll find split-image focusing screens of no value with lenses this long.*

range as follows: 200mm f/4—4'9"; 400mm f/4.5—1'4"; 600mm f/5.6—8⅝". Stopping down to f/22, the range increases in this manner: 200mm f/4—28'4"; 400mm f/4.5—6'6¾"; 600mm f/5.6—2'8¾". It thus becomes apparent that absolute accuracy in focusing is required as you climb the focal length ladder if the resulting negatives or slides are to be sufficiently sharp. There's also a creative use to which this limited depth of field can be put, and we'll discuss that shortly.

Focusing with the longer focal length telephotos presents other problems peculiar to the use of long lenses. Because of its extremely narrow angle of view, simply framing a moving object with a telephoto lens can present considerable difficulty. Once you have it located in the viewfinder, focusing accurately on the object is no easier, as it's quite likely to move completely out of range, or even become lost behind a distant obstacle you hadn't noticed before. At this point, you have to start all over and find it again, if it isn't too late to get the shot you wanted. While the object may not appear to be moving rapidly when seen with the naked eye, don't forget that distance and viewpoint have a distinct bearing on the appearance of motion. Watch a jetliner cross the sky traveling at 600 mph, yet it hardly appears to be moving until you train a 1000mm lens on it. At this point, you'll be surprised at just how much trouble you'll have keeping it in the viewfinder.

In such cases, it may be necessary to focus on a point at which you know the object will pass and then release the shutter just as it reaches the prefocused point. But this technique may well introduce still another problem—subject movement. As the object *appears* to be moving slowly when seen with the naked eye, you can easily be fooled into selecting a shutter speed that's insufficient to capture it without some degree of blurring.

It may be wiser to combine the technique of prefocusing with that of panning—picking up the object in the viewfinder and then following its progress by swinging or panning the camera in the direction of its movement. You release the shutter once it reaches the prefocused point, but continue the panning motion in a sort of follow through. If you fail to follow through, it's quite possible that you'll bring the panning motion to a halt just as you trip the shutter. If this happens, all of your effort will have been wasted, as the subject will be just as blurred as if you

12/telephoto photography

200 MM

Object Distance	f/4	f/5.6	f/8	f/11	f/16	f/22
∞ (ft)	985' –∞	704' –∞	493' –∞	359' –∞	247' –∞	180 –∞
100	91'0" –111'	87'11" –114'	83'7" –125'	78'9" –137'	71'9" –166'	65'0" –220'
70	65'6" –75'1"	63'11" –77'5"	61'7" –81'1"	59'0" –84'1"	55'1" –96'4"	51'0" –112'
50	47'9" –52'6"	46'10" –53'7"	45'8" –55'3"	44'2" –56'8"	42'0" –61'11"	39'8" –68'0"
40	38'7" –41'7"	38'0" –42'3"	37'3" –43'3"	36'3" –44'8"	34'9" –46'2"	33'2" –50'6"
30	29'2" –30'10"	28'11" –31'3"	28'5" –31'9"	27'11" –32'6"	27'0" –33'9"	26'1" –34'9"
25	24'6" –25'7"	24'3" –25'10"	23'11" –26'2"	23'7" –26'8"	22'11" –27'6"	22'3" –28'7"
15	14'10" –15'2"	14'9" –15'3"	14'8" –15'5"	14'6" –15'6"	14'4" –15'9"	14'1" –16'1"
10	9'11⅛" –10'1"	9'10¾" –10'1"	9'10¼" –10'2"	9'9⅝" –10'3"	9'8⅝" –10'4"	9'7⅜" –10'5"

400 MM

Object Distance	f/4.5	f/5.6	f/8	f/11	f/16	f/22
∞ (ft)	3,500' –∞	2,810' –∞	1,970' –∞	1,430' –∞	984' –∞	715' –∞
300	276'6½" –327'9⅞"	271'4⅛" –335'5¼"	260'8⅛" –353'4⅛"	248'5⅝" –378'7⅜"	230'5¾" –429'10½"	212'¾" –513'3½"
150	143'11⅝" –156'6⅞"	142'6¾" –158'3⅛"	139'7⅛" –162'1⅛"	136'⅝" –167'1⅞"	130'6½" –176'4⅛"	124'5⅞" –188'9⅜"
100	97'3¾" –102'10⅛"	96'8⅛" –103'6¾"	95'3¾" –105'2⅛"	93'8" –107'3⅛"	91'⅝" –110'11⅛"	88'1¼" –115'7⅞"
70	68'8¼" –71'4⅜"	68'4½" –71'8⅜"	67'8½" –72'5½"	66'10⅝" –73'5⅛"	65'6¾" –75'1⅛"	64'⅜" –77'2½"
50	49'4⅛" –50'8⅛"	49'2¼" –50'10⅛"	48'10⅛" –51'2⅝"	48'5" –51'8¼"	47'8⅞" –52'6"	46'11¼" –53'6"
40	39'7" –40'5⅛"	39'5⅞" –40'6⅜"	39'3¼" –40'9⅛'	38'11⅞" –41'⅝"	38'6¾" –41'6⅝"	38'⅝" –42'2⅛"
30	29'9¼" –30'2¾"	29'8⅝" –30'3½"	29'7⅛" –30'5"	29'5⅜" –30'6⅞"	29'2½" –30'10⅛"	28'11" –31'2"
25	24'10⅛" –25'1⅞"	24'9¾" –25'2⅜"	24'8¾" –25'3⅜"	24'7½" –25'4⅝"	24'5½" –25'6¾"	24'3⅛" –25'9⅜"
20	19'10⅞" –20'1⅛"	19'10⅝" –20'1⅜"	19'9⅞" –20'2⅛"	19'9¼" –20'2⅞"	19'7⅞" –20'4⅛"	19'6½" –20'5¾"
16	15'11¼" –16'¾"	15'11⅛" –16'⅞"	15'10¾" –16'1¼"	15'10⅜" –16'1¾"	15'9½" –16'2½"	15'8⅝" –16'3½"

600 MM

Object Distance	f/5.6	f/8	f/11	f/16	f/22
∞ (ft)	6,330' –∞	4,430' –∞	3,220' –∞	2,210' –∞	1,610' –∞
600	548'5½" –662'3¼"	528'11¾" –693'1½"	506'6" –735'11⅞"	473'⅛" –820'7⅜"	438'3⅛" –952'⅛"
300	286'8¼" –314'7⅜"	281'4" –321'4⅛"	274'11⅛" –330'1¾"	264'10½" –345'11⅝"	253'8⅞" –367'1⅛"
200	194'⅝" –206'3⅞"	191'7⅜" –209'1⅞"	188'7⅞" –212'9¾"	183'10⅞" –219'2½"	178'6⅜" –227'5"
150	146'7⅞" –153'5⅞"	145'3⅜" –155'½"	143'7⅞" –157'¼"	140'10¼" –160'5¼"	137'8½" –164'8⅞"
100	98'6½" –101'6⅛"	97'11⅛" –102'2"	97'2" –103'⅛"	95'11¼" –104'5⅛"	94"5⅞" –106'2⅜"
70	693'⅝" –70'8⅝"	69'⅛" –71'¼"	68'7⅜" –71'5⅛"	68'½" –72'1"	67'3⅞" –72'10¾"
50	49'7⅞" –50'4¼"	49'6⅛" –50'6⅛"	49'3⅞" –50'8¼"	49'⅜" –51'⅛"	48'8⅛" –51'4⅞"
40	39'9½" 40'2⅝"	39'8⅜" –40'3¾"	39'7" –40'5⅛"	39'4¾" –40'7½"	39'2⅛" –40'10⅜"
35	34'10⅛" –35'1⅞"	34'9¼" –35'2¾"	34'8¼" –35'3¾"	34'6⅝" –35'5½"	34'4⅝" –35'7⅝"

FIGURE B

hadn't bothered to pan at all.

When performed smoothly and in a proper manner, the prefocus/pan technique will permit hand-holding the camera and telephoto lens at a slower than usual shutter speed, while delivering an acceptably sharp image. To take advantage of these benefits, you must hold the camera correctly while swinging the upper part of your body in a single motion, pivoting at the hips instead of moving just your head and arms. Think of it as if someone had partially wound you up—when you begin following the action, you're unwinding your body in a smooth, continuous motion.

CAMERA MOVEMENT

For 35mm camera users, telephoto focal lengths through 135mm should present only slight problems with camera movement. Most of us can hand-hold a camera and telephoto lens of this size by using some caution in bracing ourselves and/or the camera, and keeping the shutter speed at 1/250 second or higher whenever possible. But focal lengths longer than 135mm require serious consideration on the part of the photographer to prevent image degradation from camera movement during exposure.

Regardless of how hard you try to avoid it, a certain amount of camera movement is inevitable whenever you take a picture without using the camera on a tripod. But most of us are sufficiently steady in working with a camera to keep such movement to a minimum, and it does not show up in the finished picture, at least not to the point of being noticeable or objectionable. But replacing the camera's 50mm lens with a 500mm telephoto not only increases the image size by a magnification of 10 times, it also means that any camera movement will also be magnified on the film by the same 10X factor.

If you haven't had occasion to use a really long telephoto lens before, look at it this way—the average 35mm camera body weighs 1½-2 pounds without a lens. It's nicely balanced and even adding the extra ½-pound and four-inch protrusion of a 50mm lens does not greatly upset this balance. True, the package is sufficiently heavy for some, but even so, it can be easily hand-held at shutter speeds down to 1/30 second without great difficulty. But exchange that ½-pound normal lens for a 500mm telephoto that weighs some seven pounds and you also extend the length of the lens an additional 10 inches or so beyond that of the 50mm lens. Now we're talking about holding an awkward package weighing 8½-9 pounds up to our eye long enough to focus, compose and expose a picture. Not only is this amount of weight excessive, but the entire camera/lens assembly is now very poorly balanced and virtually unmanageable in some cases. Such bulk encourages camera movement, and the harder you try to hold it steady, the more pronounced the movement seems to become.

Obviously, if you must hand-hold a long telephoto, the most logical precaution you can take to avoid camera movement is the use of the fastest shutter speed possible. But this poses other problems, as you must offset the briefer shutter speed by using a larger aperture, and this means less depth of field. Unfortunately, the particular subject in question and its distance from the camera may dictate the use of a *smaller* lens opening in order to assure an adequate range of sharpness, which leaves no alternative than to consider the other variable at your disposal—the use of a faster film, which will compensate for the lens/shutter combination you must use.

The more sensitive a film is to light, the "faster" it is. The faster the film, the higher the shutter speed and/or the smaller the lens opening you can use under a given set of conditions. So should you always use the fastest possible film when working with long focal length lenses? Not

14/telephoto photography

1. Camera movement is evident in this 800mm photograph by Ron Berkenblitt, but it also demonstrates two other qualities of the long focal length lens in an interesting composition. Space compression brought the top of a distant building almost into the foreground, while the difference in contrast shows the effect of atmospheric haze and pollution on telephotography.
2-3. A less creative but more powerful demonstration of the contrast loss in telephotography is shown in this 50mm view of the Los Angeles skyline (2). Switch to a 1000mm and the result is (3). No amount of filtration will improve your results under such conditions.
4. Newer optics like the 3⅛-inch Vivitar Series 1 800mm f/11 Solid Cat offer quality and hand-holdability, but at a substantial price.

necessarily—while this alternative makes sense at first glance, you should not overlook two very important aspects of fast films: They display grain in a more noticeable manner and tend to be inherently lower in contrast than the slower films. While it's true that grain can be minimized to some extent by development, it's difficult to compensate at the same time for the film's reduced contrast, as a lack of subject contrast is also a fact of life in telephoto photography. So before making any recommendations as to the most appropriate film speed for general usage, let's examine that characteristic.

ATMOSPHERIC INTERFERENCE

Pictures taken with longer focal length lenses often contain lightened shadows and degraded highlights—in short, they lack sufficient contrast. Why? Primarily because the atmosphere through which you're shooting acts in a manner similar to that of a diffusing screen. Such diffusion is caused by the scattering of light rays due to particles of dust, dirt, smog and other contamination contained in the atmosphere (often called aerial haze), and may be as bad on a bright, sunny day as on one that's overcast. While haze is not a problem of consequence when working with a moderate telephoto or shorter focal length, photographing a subject over a considerable distance makes it quite apparent that the air we breathe is not 100 percent pure.

Air turbulence is still another culprit that plagues long-range photography. Look across a road from a distance on a hot day and you'll see the shimmering waves—this phenomenon can pose real problems when you're working with long telephotos during hot weather. There's no real cure or shortcut around this problem, other than using a shorter focal length lens and moving closer to your subject. Although many will consider the effect of air turbulence as an insurmountable nuisance, the creative photographer will explore its use in adding feeling to his picture, especially if he's working in color photography.

As we know that light rays with short wave lengths are scattered more severely than those with long wave lengths, it's possible to offset the tendency toward aerial haze diffusion (but not air turbulence) by using a filter to reduce its effect on the film. As blue light is the greatest offender (shortest wave length), the amount of it reaching the film is reduced somewhat by using a yellow filter. To reduce its effect even further, change to an orange filter—a red one will maximize the reduction possible and increase subject contrast considerably. The so-called UV or Haze filters are useless in black-and-white photography; their primary value is in reducing the bluish cast which excessive ultraviolet rays cause on color film.

But at this point, you're resting on the horn of dilemma again. In order to use a yellow (2X), orange (4X) or red (8X) filter, you must increase exposure by one, two or three f-stops to compensate for the reduction in the amount of light reaching the film. So if you select a fast film to permit the use of a higher shutter speed while retaining the smaller aperture, the use of a filter to enhance the lowered contrast inherent in the scene and the film puts you right back where you started. It thus becomes a compromise situation regardless of how you turn, dependent to a large extent upon your subject and how you wish it rendered on the film. If contrast is of maximum importance in long-range photography, you might even use an infrared emulsion such as Kodak High Speed Infrared film. Properly filtered, this film has perhaps the best haze-cutting properties obtainable.

Generally speaking, you'll probably need an ASA 400 black-and-white emulsion when hand-holding the longer telephoto lenses, along with a filter. If you're working in color, you'll want a film speed in the ASA 160-200 range, combined with a UV or Skylight filter to cut down on the bluish effect of haze. Use the fastest shutter speed practical to increase the possibility that your results will be satisfactory and you'll have

1. done everything possible to make those hand-held shots a success.

There is one other option I should mention at this time. Should you envision more than occasional hand-holding of long telephoto shots, you might well consider the use of a mirror lens instead of the standard optical glass type. Because of its considerably reduced size and weight (which we'll consider at length in the chapter devoted to them), the mirror lens has distinct advantages not possessed by the glass lens.

As we've seen, incorrect focusing, camera movement and atmospheric interference all have the potential to degrade the quality of your pictures taken with longer focal length lenses. While the first two factors can affect your pictures regardless of the lens used, atmospheric interference does not usually become a subject for concern until you reach the 400mm and longer lenses. But all of these factors can be overcome, or at least sufficiently minimized, by practicing the proper techniques of focusing and holding the camera, using a tripod or other camera support whenever possible, and by a judicious choice of film, filter and developer combination relative to the subject and its desired treatment. There are, however, two very important creative aspects involved in

1. *A medium focal length telephoto combined with the use of fast film can put you where the action is—in this case, right beside an aerial act at the Ringling Brothers and Barnum and Bailey circus.*
2-3. *The telephoto's ability to compress perspective can be put to use creatively. Ken Moore used a 300mm for the whimsical tail-to-tail shot at Dulles International (2), while Jeff Blackwell created a scene of intense activity where there was none by stacking up sailboats along the beach (3).*

using a telephoto lens with which you should be conversant before we move into a consideration of each focal length range, its peculiarities and most suitable applications.

SPACE COMPRESSION

The first is a compression of distance, which increases in effect as the focal length increases. This makes objects at all planes in the field of view appear much closer to each other than they really are. You can always distinguish a picture taken with a 1000mm lens from that made with a 135mm, as the background appears large, with little or no separation between objects which you know are really quite distant from each other. Thus long focal length lenses draw things together

and toward the camera in a manner the human eye cannot accomplish by itself. This is evident in photographed sports—watch a televised baseball game with the camera positioned behind home plate and it's hard to believe that 60 feet actually separate the pitcher and batter from each other. Compression is also a favorite technique of TV news cameramen when covering subjects like traffic congestion—point a long lens at a moderately crowded highway and you'll pack the cars so thickly that they appear to merge into one another.

What we're talking about is really nothing more than a case of relative sizes—our old friend apparent perspective again. You expect distant objects to be smaller in scale than those close to you, and that's how the camera's normal lens reproduces them. But use a long telephoto lens and back away from those close objects until their image size on the film equals that produced by the 50mm lens, and the distant objects in the scene suddenly appear much larger, as well as much closer to the nearby ones.

Remember that subject distance and camera angle are the controlling factors in this use of perspective. The more distant the subject is from the camera, the less the effect will be noticed. In such cases, there is a tendency to lose the feeling of distance between near and far objects when both are a considerable distance from the camera. But with a little thought, you can put this compression of space to work for you creatively. Add impact by approaching your primary subject from a close viewpoint and it will loom large, overshadowing its background—or adopt a low viewpoint to dramatize the leap of an athlete. Use your imagination (i.e., creativity) with virtually any subject and you can create *different* pictures.

SHALLOW DEPTH

Earlier, we discussed the necessity for accurate

focusing with the longer telephotos because of the shallow depth-of-field characteristic of such lenses. This shallow depth should be regarded not as a limitation of the lens but rather as a creative tool which offers you the ability to direct interest on your subject without the distraction of a jumbled foreground or cluttered background. Of course, in order to put this tool to work in the most effective manner, you must be able to choose and use the right focal length lens, as well as select the proper camera-subject distance and aperture that will produce the desired amount of shallowness in depth. This requires some degree of familiarity (practice) with the lenses you have at hand.

Incidentally, since the effects of both shallow depth and space compression are greatest at the closer camera-to-subject distances, don't fall into the trap of reaching for a telephoto only when you're working with distant subjects. There's a good deal of use for them at distances between 10 and 50 feet other than simply allowing you to shoot without your subject's knowledge. To give you an idea of the many and varied practical uses for the various focal length ranges, as well as some hints about selecting the right ones for your requirements, the following chapters treat each range individually. If you're ready, let's step into the exciting world of telephotography—lens by lens. □

telephoto photography/17

85-105mm

This focal length range contains the "moderate" telephotos for 35mm camera users—85mm, 90mm, 100mm and 105mm. Only slightly larger in size and bulk than the normal 50-58mm lenses fitted to SLR bodies (although often considerably heavier), most 85mm lenses range from f/1.4 to f/2.8 in speed, providing almost the same degree of available-light capability. Rangefinder camera users will find the 90mm focal length peculiar to their camera type—only one lens in that particular focal length is offered for SLR use—and need not look for the others, as they're not offered for rangefinder cameras.

If you stay with the lens line offered by the manufacturer of your camera body, the 85mm will generally use the same size filter as your normal lens; those offered by independent manufacturers will usually require a filter one or two sizes larger because the optical formula is a compromise that works with several different bodies.

For most, the 85mm makes an ideal focal length with which to experience the initial feel of telephotography. It offers approximately 1.7X magnification over the normal 50mm, while penalizing you only slightly in terms of speed and loss of depth. Many pros who use the 35mm as their basic lens also favor the 85mm—in this case, the magnification ratio becomes 2.4X and thus gives the 85mm a significant reach. It's also an excellent choice for portrait work, as the extra distance between camera and subject reduces the ungainly perspective often caused when you bring a 35mm or 50mm too close to your subject.

Its speed is generally sufficient for indoor photography with existing illumination, and because the 85mm is not much larger than a 50mm, many subjects will not realize that you're pointing a telephoto in their direction. For this reason, you're not likely to draw unwanted attention or undue interest should they notice you and the camera. Thus you can stay close enough to the action to keep abreast of what's going on, work verbally with your subjects if necessary, and yet remain relatively unobtrusive should the situation dictate that you stay out of the mainstream.

In terms of image size, you'll get a more distinct telephoto "feel" from the 100-105mm lenses, which provide a 2X and 2.1X magnification, respectively, over the 50mm. Generally speaking, your camera manufacturer will offer one, but not both of these focal lengths; if you have one, the other is not necessary, as their effect is not materially different. Which one is

1. Moderate telephotos can be combined with longer ones to create perspective doubletakes. This multiple exposure was made with a 100mm and a 400mm. (Ron Berkenblitt.)
2. While many prefer the longer 105-135mm telephotos, the 85mm is also an ideal portrait lens. (Ron Berkenblitt.)

Moving into this focal length bracket offers several definitive advantages. It provides an ideal depth-of-field range, from shallow depth at maximum to considerable depth at minimum aperture. Focusing on a point 20 feet distant at f/2.5, you'll have approximately 21 inches of sharpness, but stop down to f/22 and this expands to slightly over 18 feet! Combine this with its 20-19-degree horizontal angle of view, and you can treat backgrounds selectively simply by choice of aperture.

Sufficiently fast for most work under existing illumination (especially when combined with a faster emulsion), these short and comparatively lightweight optics (many are lighter than their 85mm brethren) have a wide variety of uses—they'll let you pick a single figure out of a crowd 25-30 feet away, or fill the frame with a head shot from six or seven feet, making the 100-105mm equally handy for portraits without crowding in on your subject. In addition, they have just enough reach to make them useful to those who are interested in such specialized areas as nature and sports photography.

It's at this upper end of the moderate telephoto range that you first begin to notice radical changes in the appearance of subjects in your viewfinder, and can start to educate your eye both to the telephoto effect, and to the task of selecting significant details from the visual jumble which your eye sees. Along with these virtues, the 100-105mm will force you to dispense with a good deal of unnecessary detail, cropping your pictures in the camera to record only the bare essentials of the subject.

Many who photograph pets and children actually prefer the 100-105mm focal length over other options, as they provide sufficient

provided to fit your camera will depend to a large extent upon the manufacturer's philosophy toward his lens offerings—the 105mm is a more "traditional" focal length, while the 100mm is usually offered by those who work in multiples of the standard lens—50mm, 100mm, 150mm, etc. For the most part, maximum lens speed is f/2.5 or f/2.8, and here also the required filter size should be the same as, or at the most, one size larger than that used with the 50mm.

working distance between camera and subject to avoid annoying the subject or causing self-consciousness, yet like the 85mm, do not separate yourself so far from the scene that you lose total control over what takes place in your viewfinder.

The beauty of both ends of this moderate telephoto range rests in the fact that whether you have an 85mm, a 100-105mm, or both, they are eminently useful lenses in general photography. Unlike the longer focal lengths, they are not sufficiently powerful to become highly specialized in use, nor is their speed so slow as to require the use of a tripod or other camera support to assure sharp images. Much of your work can still be done with a slow- or medium-speed film, and filters can be used without worrying about having to slow the shutter speed excessively. In addition, these lenses usually focus to 3½-4 feet, relatively close for a telephoto, and so allow you to work fairly close to your subject if necessary.

Because of their comparatively small size and weight, either end of this focal length spectrum can be used for sharp hand-held pictures, with only a minor modification required in your technique, if any. Depending upon the particular lens in question—the moderate telephotos vary somewhat in length and weight—it's well to rest the left hand under the lens for support when focusing and shooting. This braces the lens somewhat to make steady shooting as easy as with the normal lens, and most people should be able to hand-hold the 105mm down to 1/60 second without difficulty.

If you're into using trick filters and lens attachments, you should consider the 85mm as the ultimate focal length for their effective use. Even at that, there are some subjects with which many such attachments won't work very well, and with others, the camera-to-subject distance will become critical if you wish to record complete images. Use of prism or multiple-image attachments containing more than three sections is not advisable—you'll have your best luck with the three-section parallel or triangular designs.

Those readers with a sneaky bend of mind may well have already concluded that the moderate telephoto can be a handy "cheater" for certain types of electronic flash photography. Suppose that you're using a nonautomatic flash with an ASA 25 guide number of 40, your camera is loaded with ASA 400 film, and your normal lens will only stop down to f/16. As your flash guide number with this particular combination is 160, you can come no closer to your subject than 10 feet, without using some means of reducing the illumination from your flash unit. But switch to a 100-105mm and you can *double* the size of the image on your film from your minimum flash position. In fact, you can double the image size from any position along the flash range.

Of course, you're losing the use of a large part of the total flash output; at a minimum, most electronic flash units are designed to spread their illumination over the field of view equivalent to that of a 35mm lens. A recent trend in electronic flash design has been plastic snap-on wide-angle lenses and diffusers to further spread the light output for use with 28mm and even 24mm lenses—but at a shorter effective flash range.

Automatic electronic flash units equipped with such broad-field sensors often pose problems when using lenses longer than the 50-58mm range. As the angle of acceptance of such sensors is so much greater than the angle of view of an 85-105mm lens, it's entirely possible that objects outside the lens's field of view will cause the sensor to quench the flash output too early, resulting in underexposure. But Vivitar and Metz have recently come to the rescue, providing sensors with adjustable angles of acceptance to work with all lenses from 35mm through 105mm, and this development reflected in the Vivitar 365 and the Metz 45 CT 1 is bound to start another new trend in electronic flash design.

A similar problem in determining exposure outdoors afflicts that hardy band of photographers who favor the use of a hand-held meter over the SLR's through-the-lens metering system. Unless you own one of the expensive hand meters that allows you to vary the angle of the meter cell's acceptance, you'll get

1-2. Most moderate telephotos are sufficiently fast for available light photography. Ron Berkenblitt used a 100mm to photograph Bob Seeger performing on stage (1), and Cathy Dunbar in mid-air during the final Olympic trials for the women's gym team (2).
3. The 105mm is a good choice for photographing pets, as you can remain far enough from the subject to avoid disturbing it.
4. While it's possible to photograph action such as this racing car with the moderate telephotos, you must be fairly close to them for an image size of consequence. Ron Berkenblitt was standing right on the track with his 105mm as the cars zipped by.

a reading which represents the meter's considered opinion about an area that's at least twice as large as that seen by your lens. Depending upon the area your lens sees, and its relative influence in the overall area seen by the meter, the resulting exposure recommendation may be off by an f-stop or more.

Fortunately, this problem does not exist for those who rely on their in-camera meter, as its angle of acceptance changes automatically with the lens used. With some tricky subjects, however, there may be a one-third to one-half stop variation in exposure depending upon the type of metering system provided—averaging or center-weighted. If your camera is one of the few to offer the option of a spot reading as well, you'll find this quite useful at times.

So which focal length should you buy first—the 85mm or a 100-105mm? A reasonable enough question, but one which only you can really answer, as both lenses have definite advantages, especially if your camera manufacturer offers the 105mm instead of the 100mm—that extra 5mm in focal length really makes the 105mm a far more useful lens when you already have an 85mm.

It's often suggested that a good beginning approach in putting together a battery of telephoto lenses is to pass over every other focal length above that of your normal lens. Thus, if you have an 85mm, you'll skip the 100-105mm and go directly to the 135mm; if you have the 100mm or 105mm, you'll bypass the 135-150mm and go directly to the longer 180-200mm range.

For those who have one of the short zooms, such as the 43-86mm Nikkor or 35-70mm Canon, the choice of a 100-105mm is obvious, but if you have no lenses other than the one furnished with your camera body, my personal recommendation is for a high-speed 85mm, which will let you reach out to subjects without materially changing your shooting habits at the present. If you can afford a 105mm in addition, it's a very useful lens and one you won't regret owning. So if skipping every other focal length seems to make sense to you, I'd suggest that you begin it after acquiring a 135-150mm. Of course, basic to this decision is your regard toward the zoom lens concept; if you are captivated by the zoom and its potential, three of them will cover the 50-600mm range and there's no need to make a decision about individual focal lengths. Thus, I'd suggest that you resolve this question first before investing very much money in individual focal lengths. □

120-150mm

Easily the most popular telephoto focal length range, and usually the first accessory lens bought by amateurs, there are well over a hundred 135mm lenses available for 35mm cameras, but only two currently provided in the 120mm length and a half-dozen 150mm lenses. Almost every camera manufacturer as well as independent lens line offers at least two 135mm telephotos—an economy and a top-of-the-line model. How do they differ other than price? Primarily in optical formula used, lens speed and quality of mechanical construction. The best 135mm lenses generally contain 5-6 elements arranged in 4-5 groups, have a close-focusing point somewhere between five and eight feet, and provide an aperture range from f/2.8 to f/22. Their companion economy versions are usually designed with one less element arranged in one or possibly two less groups, focus to the same 5-8 feet, and have a maximum aperture of f/3.5. A few of the independent optics have been designed with an f/1.8 aperture, but these are massive hunks of glass, both in diameter and in weight—one well-known brand typical of all such high-speed 135mm telephotos weighs 1¾ pounds (as much as most camera bodies alone) and requires the use of an 82mm filter.

Compared to the 100-105mm, most well-designed 135mm optics will weigh some 3-6 ounces more, are approximately ⅝ to 1¼ inches longer, but should use the same size filter, although it's not unusual to find that the faster version will require the use of a filter one size larger than its slower companion. This comparative light weight and short length make the 120-150mm lenses fairly easy to carry, and only slightly more difficult to hand-hold than the 100-105mm optics. But for sharpest results, you should plan on using a shutter speed sufficiently fast to eliminate any possible camera movement. Remember, the 2.7X magnification means that any camera shake will also be magnified to the same degree.

There's an old rule of thumb which states that you should work with a shutter speed at least equal to the focal length of the lens in use. Following this rule means setting 1/125 second as your minimum speed, but unless you have one of the new breed of really small telephotos, I'd recommend that you work at 1/250 second, at least until you acquire some experience in handling the 120-150mm lenses without difficulty.

While it's natural to expect that the more complicated the optical formula, the sharper the pictures, this is not always true—much depends upon how the manufacturer designs his lenses and what size pictures you expect to produce. Often, both versions will give comparable results up to a certain point, at which one then becomes superior to the other if further enlargement is desired. Unfortunately, you can't always depend upon brand name and price difference to tell you which one is superior—with one well-known brand favored by many professionals, the f/3.5 clearly has the edge over the more expensive f/2.8 version.

When it comes to selecting between the two, you would

1. The 135mm is ideal for those times when you need that little extra reach which the 85mm lacks. Hal Stoelzle caught this parachute jumper at just the right moment without having to crop the negative.
2. Shooting this figure study with a 135mm, Ron Berkenblitt was able to put sufficient distance between model and camera to avoid any apparent perspective distortion of the linear form.

do well to consider exactly what uses you envision for the 135mm and then ask yourself if the extra ⅔ f-stop is really worth the additional money asked, as well as the possible inferior performance at certain points along the f-stop and focusing ranges. As the slower 135mm will prove more than adequate for general work in most cases, I'd advise the purchase of the faster f/2.8 version only if you absolutely need the slight increase in speed for existing-light photography. As for the high-speed f/1.8 lenses, you'll find that their increased speed will extract its payment in picture quality, especially in the fall off of sharpness from the picture center to its edges. For the majority of work, you'd stop down to f/5.6 or smaller anyway, so paying the price in cash and quality loss is rather foolish unless you do a good deal of theatre, stage or other such existing-light photography where simply capturing the image is of utmost importance and not much attention will be paid to the edges of the resulting pictures. Even then, the extra weight and bulk of such lenses make a consideration of faster film and/or push processing techniques a viable option.

If you're the curious type, you're probably wondering why there is such a vast choice of 135mm lenses available. Consider this—of all the longer than normal focal length lenses, this particular one is undoubtedly the most versatile. It will handle fairly distant subjects with reasonable aplomb while producing excellent results with close-ups, portraits, sporting events, landscapes, etc. You name it and the 135mm will give you more than a fighting chance of bringing it back on film, and with a touch of flair. Let's see why.

For openers, the 135mm has just about the right amount of "reach" for an all-around telephoto, and without the vices of the longer focal lengths. As a portrait lens, you can fill the frame from a distance of 10 feet; for candid work, a person fills the negative from 30 feet away. The effect of space compression on various planes of distance first becomes really noticeable at this focal length, which provides perhaps the best compromise between normal lens and long telephoto. Focus on that person at 30 feet and you'll have slightly more than three feet of acceptable sharpness with the f/3.5 lens wide open; close it down to f/8 and the range expands to almost eight feet; close it all the way to f/22 and you virtually triple the sharpness range. Yet the 135mm does have its limitations—at wide open aperture (f/3.5) and its closest focusing point (five feet), the lens will give but a 1¼-inch range of sharpness.

For many years now, studio photographers have relied upon the use of long focal length lenses for portrait work, and you can take advantage of their expertise with a 135mm. One of their "tricks of the trade" revolves around the perspective effect provided by such optics. As we know, approaching a person at a point close enough to fill the negative with a "head and shoulders" portrait using a normal lens (3½-4 feet) causes an unpleasant distortion of features. But using a 135mm in the same situation allows you to increase your camera distance from the subject sufficiently to eliminate such undesirable effects. At the same time, moving the camera away from the subject gives you an opportunity to light the subject in a more professional manner, and is especially desirable when you're limited to the use of on-camera flash. Bounce lighting is also more effective for such pictures when used in conjunction with a 135mm instead of the 50mm lens.

Our 135mm is also a highly useful focal length when it comes to sports and action photography. It will do the same job at 54 feet that the 50mm does at 20 feet, is more easily hand-held than longer telephotos, and solves the problem of getting you close enough to the action to capture that intimate feeling of competition without actually interferring with what's going on. The

telephoto photography/23

135mm will get you into the center of a football play, let you pick up the drama of a double play from the third base line, or isolate a racing car from the rest of the pack. Thus you can record the emotions and expressions of individual competitors, revealing the excitement and inherent drama of actually "being" there, which the casual observer cannot see with the naked eye.

Animal and pet photographs benefit from use of the 135mm in much the same way. In addition to keeping you far enough from the subject to prevent interference with normal actions and behavior patterns, the resulting pictures are far more natural in appearance. Keeping your distance from a playful animal, such as a kitten toying with a ball of yarn, lets you select the most appropriate angle and viewpoint, while providing a sufficient amount of background control (by aperture selection) to prevent it from distracting visually from your subject.

Similar benefits are obtained from using the 135mm for close-up work—those flower fanciers who wish to record their special blooms will find the 135mm ideal from the advantages of perspective and background control, as well as in creating lighting effects. Coming in too close to such subjects when utilizing natural lighting can make the choice of viewpoint dependent upon a position where you won't cast unwanted shadows over the subject. But back off to the 135mm's closest focusing point and fit a +1, +2 or +3 close-up attachment to the lens, and virtually any camera position can be used without fear of shadows. This particular trick will also prove useful to those who wish to photograph birds, insects and other wildlife in their natural habitat.

1. The 135mm and a touch of diffusion combine to make an effective portrait. Again, camera-to-subject distance is helpful in avoiding disproportionate emphasis of facial features. (Ron Berkenblitt.)
2. Some slight the 135mm for not having sufficient reach, but Glenn Cooper found it perfect here. There's just enough magnification to frame the bird effectively, while throwing the background out of focus to center the eye's interest.
3. There are some subjects which you simply cannot get close to, and that's the time to have a 135mm handy. While it may not deliver as large an image as you'd like, it will retain image size while letting you put almost three times the distance between you and the subject. (Ron Berkenblitt.)
4. There are even times when the 135mm's in-camera cropping ability makes it a more useful focal length than that generally used with such subjects, as in Hal Stoelzle's moody interpretation of man's mad rush toward pollution—via freeway.

Incidentally, Sigma now offers a lens in this focal length with the ability to stop down to f/64. Known as its "Pantel" feature (which will probably be extended to other Sigma lenses and may well be adopted by other manufacturers), this lens has an additional click stop beyond f/22 on the aperture ring. Setting the ring to this marked "PAN/64" position closes the aperture down in one step to f/64, resulting in an enormous increase in depth of field.

The Pantel feature works automatically with stop-down metering systems, but cameras using open-aperture metering do not have meter coupling pins capable of reading down to f/64. Thus the correct exposure must be set manually by slowing

the shutter speed down three increments beyond the correct exposure indicated for use at f/22. This feature should prove desirable for a variety of applications, including landscapes and scenics.

Landscapes and scenics with the 135mm—why not? In addition to their usefulness in transcending distance and space limitations over which you have little, if any control, there are a wide variety of uses for this focal length—you can pull in branches of a tree to act as a pictorial frame, accentuate a long wooden fence such as those still used in New England, eliminate superfluous or extraneous material from your viewpoint, change background relationships with your primary subject—the list is virtually endless.

The 135mm is also useful for those who want to move beyond the stage of "reach out and bring close" photography. As well as the more obvious applications I've already brought to your attention, this focal length can open an entirely new visual world for those interested in exploring the unlimited potential that most subjects offer the creative photographer. Point your telephoto into the street from a high vantage point, look for the patterns created by buildings along a street, or skyline shots of the city at dusk. Look for texture, lines and patterns in nature that can be isolated and amplified. Try putting the flatter perspective of the 135mm to use, shooting identical objects in such a way as to retain their relative proportions—with the 135mm, the world's your oyster.

Do you need a 135mm if you already have a 100-105mm telephoto? I would recommend that everyone interested in telephotography acquire the 85mm, 105mm and 135mm, in that order, but unfortunately, many shoot for the 135mm first and then move into the 85-210mm (or nearest equivalent) zoom lens without acquiring the self-discipline in visualizing subjects which my suggested focal length selections impose. Incidentally, Pentax owners would do well to consider the 120mm f/2.8 and 150mm f/4 lenses offered for their cameras as possible alternatives for the 105mm and 135mm, especially if they do not anticipate moving into the longer focal lengths. The 120mm carries you sufficiently beyond the 85mm to make a real difference, and the 150mm has nearly all the virtues of the 135mm, while actually weighing less, with only a fractional sacrifice in speed.

Whether you use the 135mm just to pull your subject or a part of it in closer to you, or for some specialized use such as photographing products to retain proper perspective of their right angles, it's probably the most useful telephoto lens you'll acquire, and the one you'll reach for most often once you've learned its true value to your work. But for those interested in bigger and better things, it's time to move along and look at what are often called the "action" telephotos. □

180-300mm

Moving into this focal length range, you'll see radical differences when you look through the viewfinder. While there are six different stops along the way from 180mm to 300mm—180, 200, 210, 250, 280 and 300mm—the most popular seems to be the 200mm, with approximately one-half the number of 135mm optics available in this focal length, or more than 60 from which to choose. This is followed in popularity by the 300mm, which provides almost as wide a selection, and the 180mm, with a dozen offerings. The scattering of lenses in the 210, 250 and 280mm focal lengths are specifically designed for use with particular cameras, especially the rangefinder types where a housing is used to convert its viewing system from eye-level to through-the-lens.

As the focal length jumps between 135mm, 180-200mm and 300mm are considerable, image magnification increases proportionately (3.6X, 4X, 6X), with decreasing depth of field, and far more noticeable alteration in the apparent perspective than found in the less significant steps between the shorter telephotos we've already discussed. This means that if a picture is made with a 180mm lens and the negative is enlarged 10 times, you've produced an 8x10 print representing the subject 36 times larger than your eye saw it—40 times larger with the 200mm and 60 times if the 300mm is used—and that's dramatic!

But simply increasing image size tremendously doesn't mean that you'll necessarily capture the same degree of visual excitement within the borders of that 8x10 print. It's perfectly possible (and more often likely) that you'll end up with little more than a greatly magnified visual bore, unless you have both the interest and desire to seek out the most effective uses for such potent lenses.

As the 200-300mm lenses are the most commonly offered, let's concentrate our consideration on these two focal lengths. Like the 135mm, many manufacturers offer a choice of two different lenses in the 200mm as well as the 300mm telephotos. With some independent lens lines, the difference between the two is not only one of lens speed and close-focusing point, but also in the type of diaphragm action offered. While most of these lenses can be obtained with an automatic diaphragm (like that of your other lenses), there is the less costly (and less convenient) option of selecting a manual or preset instead. What's the difference?

The manual diaphragm is operated by a single control ring, which is used to open the aperture to its widest point and then turned back to the necessary f-stop setting by hand for a proper exposure before releasing the shutter. A preset diaphragm uses two control rings. One is fitted with f-stop numbers and click-stop detents, while the other ring turns freely to open and close the aperture along its entire range. To use, the first ring is "preset" at the aperture required for correct exposure, then the second ring is used to open the diaphragm for focusing and viewing. When you're ready to take your picture, you turn the second ring until it stops against the aperture setting preset by the first ring. This semiautomation of the preset lens makes it unnecessary for you to remove your eye from the viewfinder prior to exposure in order to accurately find the correct f-stop setting. Both diaphragm types are far less convenient than one that is automatic, and are not really suitable for certain kinds of work such as action photography, because setting the aperture to the correct f-stop for an exposure also dims the viewfinder image sufficiently to make viewing difficult (if not impossible) under some conditions.

The 200mm telephotos range in speed from f/3.5 to f/5.6, with a few offered as fast as f/2.8, but you'll pay dearly in comparison for their extra speed. Barrel length is usually between five and seven inches, weight between one and two pounds, and filter sizes required may range up to 67mm. Considering all the available 200mm designs, the nearest point of focus can range between seven and 12 feet, but most are designed to focus to either eight or 10 feet from the camera.

A rotating tripod attachment ring around the barrel may or may not be provided, according to the manufacturer's estimation of the amount of stress his lens will put on the camera's mounting flange and tripod socket. Quality lenses of brand names which are not equipped with such a device are considered sufficiently light to hand-hold, provided you use a fast enough shutter speed—usually 1/500 second or higher—although with practice and a steady hand, or a nearby object on which you can brace the camera and lens, it's not out of the question to get sharp results at speeds as low as 1/250 second.

Move up the focal length ladder to 300mm and you'll find that lens speed ranges

1. Jeff Blackwell found a 200mm sufficient to capture California's governor Jerry Brown on the stump with Democratic candidate Jimmy Carter.
2. Using a 300mm from the Dodger dugout, sports photographer Glenn Cooper appears to be standing right beside Bill Buckner as he fouls off a pitch.

26/telephoto photography

telephoto photography/27

between f/4 and f/5.6, with at least one rated at f/2.8 offered at this writing, but again a very expensive option. The 300mm lenses are usually 7-10 inches in length, weigh somewhere between 1½ and 3½ pounds, and may require filters as large as 82mm. As a group, their closest focusing point will be found between 11 and 25 feet, but the majority of such lenses are designed to focus to a minimum of 12, 15 or 20 feet, depending upon the manufacturer.

Virtually all are fitted with some provision for tripod mounting to relieve any undue stress on the camera's tripod socket and lens mount. While some of the lighter 300mm telephotos can be hand-held under conditions similar to those discussed for 200mm lenses, it's advisable in most cases to use them with some form of camera support, whether a tripod, monopod or simply by bracing them against a solid object to minimize camera movement.

At this particular focal length, we begin to get into the use of specialty glass at premium prices, such as the fluorocrown Nikkor ED series, or the artificial fluorite crystal Canon FL optics, which are said to completely eliminate secondary spectra. Regardless of the type of lens materials used, all such special lens designs are supposed to produce the same superior optical qualities—crisper definition, excellent resolving power and elimination of color aberrations. Unfortunately, current prices for such designs are exceedingly high when compared with the more traditional designs, but they do point toward a future trend in lens design, and once quantity production can be achieved, prices will drop accordingly. Thus, it's not difficult to foresee many such telephoto lenses coming along in the next years.

What can you do with lenses from this focal length range? Those who are into wildlife or nature photography will find them especially useful, as their 1.3X-3.3X increase in magnification over that provided by the 135mm will often make the difference between obtaining a suitable image size and one that needs considerable cropping during enlargement. While the 135mm can be regarded as a good focal length for "grab shots," the 200-300mm lenses are more appropriate for those who are definitely stalking their subject, as they can be tripod-mounted in an

1. Working with a 300mm allows the photographer to remain unobtrusive. Hank Harris used it to capture this California farm worker harvesting celery. Note the narrow plane of focus which emphasizes the subject.
2. Like many others who photograph sports, Jeff Blackwell finds plenty of use for his 200mm. It has just the right amount of reach and sufficient compression effect to put you in the action.
3. To reach out to subjects which could not be approached otherwise, many rely on the 300mm. (Hank Harris.)

inconspicious place and prefocused while awaiting the appearance of your quarry.

Although the 135mm lets you isolate an action situation during various sporting events, the 200-300mm brings you right into the middle of what's going on to pick out individuals and their reactions, expressions and emotions. It's also a handy focal length range for those who cover political rallies, official meetings and disaster situations. On the one hand, they may not be allowed close enough to make effective use of less powerful optics, and on the other, a raging fire or riot may make it inadvisable from the standpoint of personal safety to approach the situation from a closer vantage point.

Don't overlook the creative potentials offered by the flattening of perspective and the more shallow depth of field prevalent with the 200-300mm lenses. You've now reached a focal length range where the world of the telephoto effect has really started to unfold and the uses to which you put one of these lenses are limited only by your own imagination—make it work for you and create out-of-the-ordinary pictures from seemingly mundane subject matter.

Obviously, the lighter weight, shorter length and closer focusing ability of the 200mm tend to give it a distinct edge over the somewhat slower and more bulky 300mm when it comes to selecting the lens best suited for your purposes. Although the 300mm is often billed as a "general-purpose super telephoto," it's considerably less helpful in spite of its greater magnification (6X instead of 4X) to the average photographer, who is unlikely to find very much use for it unless he does a good deal of wildlife, sports and news photography—all previously mentioned subjects with which it is most generally associated—or unless you've really been bitten by the creative bug. To simplify matters, the 200mm will do much the same thing that the 300mm does, but with somewhat less space compression, two-thirds the image size, and slightly more depth of field. In return for this, you'll have that extra ½-1 f-stop in lens speed.

Regardless of whether you eventually settle upon the 200mm or the 300mm as best suited for the work you

wish to do, you should carefully evaluate the available choices in terms of your anticipated needs and use for that specific focal length. To wisely invest in a 200-300mm lens, price should not really have to be a factor in your decision—if you cannot afford the lens you really need, you might as well save your money, as a lesser lens will quite likely gather dust once you've found its weaknesses.

While it may be very tempting to sacrifice the speed of a heavier lens, such as an f/3.5 weighing 31 ounces, in order to gain the lighter overall weight of an f/5.6 at 14 ounces, that greater lens speed can prove exceedingly handy when working in dim lighting conditions, shooting color film, and for focusing/viewing. At the same time, if much of your use for the lens will be outdoors under favorable lighting conditions, it's rather foolish to go for the faster and heavier lens if you're not going to make use of its greater speed, yet be handicapped to some extent by its bulk and weight.

The same sort of logic should be applied if you're tempted to settle for a manual or preset diaphragm. The automatic diaphragm will make whatever lens you buy that much more useful to you under a wider variety of conditions. But if your "thing" is collecting photographs of church steeples, and that's the primary use you envision for your 200-300mm, the choice of a preset lens may be far more appropriate from cost, speed and weight considerations than it would be to someone who's working mainly with football games and the like.

Those readers who, for one reason or another, have definitely established this focal length range as the outer limits of their telephotography interest will do well to give the 300mm serious consideration over the 200mm (providing they own a 135mm), but after reading our next chapter, if there's the slightest doubt in your mind about stopping here, go for the 200mm and make your next acquisition the big one in terms of effect. □

350-600mm

We've now entered the world of "occasional use" telephotos, where the disadvantages begin to prove overwhelming for many casual photographers. One of these long lenses can often cause longer faces after spending a day or two shooting everything in sight for the first time and then developing the film. While many users are apt to blame the lens for their sad looking negatives, the chances are very good that the reason for their disappointment rests more in faulty technique than in the optics.

Once you get into the 8-12X magnification ranges, atmospheric haze can really take its toll of contrast and definition. The resulting negatives may look sadly underdeveloped, as well as bearing all the earmarks of having been taken with a silk stocking stretched over the lens. One useful approach to the problem is that of deliberately underexposing by one f-stop and then overdeveloping the negatives by about 20 percent; another recommended solution you might find helpful is the use of a polarizing filter and an increase in development of approximately 25 percent.

Despite the many problems encountered at these more extreme magnifications, one particular focal length—the 400mm—seems to be very popular with a large number of telephoto addicts. A good part of the reason for this undue interest in that particular focal length is the fact that almost half of the 40-odd 400mm lenses available can be acquired for under $100, and several of these for less than $60. At those prices, virtually anyone can partake of the "Long Tom" or "Girl Watcher Special," as these lenses have been nicknamed.

Naturally, there has to be a reason for the low cost (which hasn't risen that much in these inflationary times), and a good part of it is explained by the use of simple achromatic doublet designs with a speed of f/5.6 or f/6.3, housed in a long metal tube, and equipped with a preset or manual diaphragm. The more expensive telephoto designs may use slightly faster and far more complex optical formulas (f/4-f/5.6), internal focusing to reduce overall length, and automatic diaphragms that couple with particular cameras, but the cost quickly rises accordingly.

As an example, Minolta owners willing to part with $1500 (list price) can acquire a seven-element, six-group 400mm f/5.6 Apo Tele Rokkor-X lens containing a fluorite element. This virtually eliminates the green light aberrations of secondary spectra which have a degrading effect on the image, and at the same time, the use of fluorite allows the three-pound 3⅞-ounce lens to be housed in a barrel only 10 3/32 inches long. The lens comes with a specially designed 2X converter of five-element, three-group construction to convert it to a very compact, high-performance 800mm f/11 super telephoto, while preserving meter coupling and automatic diaphragm operation. Obviously, there's a good deal of difference between this particular image-maker (and others like it), and the $60 "Girl Watcher Special."

So just what do you get for your money with one of the low-cost 400mm telephotos? A reasonably sharp image-maker, if you stop down a couple notches, don't plan on big enlargements, and can hold it steady during exposure (a tripod is highly recommended to prevent those long faces when the proof sheet is examined closely), but one that often shows signs of flare, considerable secondary color aberration, color fringing and residual ghosts. Yet you can't expect perfection at that price, and many of the more expensive multicoated optics of the same focal length will possess the same defects in varying amounts.

Does this mean that you should pass over an opportunity to experience the reach of a 400mm at a price you can probably afford without breaking your budget? Certainly not! While the list of defects enumerated above sounds most imposing, there's very little chance that they'll interfere with your enjoyment of such a lens, as long as you're fully aware that it *does* possess limitations. Those who are absolute perfectists, or who plan on trying to sell their work, should strive for a better lens, but for the large number of us who take pictures for our own pleasure, simple adherence to the basic rules governing successful telephotography will make the low-cost 400mm a most welcome addition to our lens kits.

At the same time you're pulling in a good close-up from the opposite end of a football field, the 500-600mm lenses will bring an increasing awareness of the problems involved in using long lenses. Your subjects will be hundreds of yards (instead of feet) away when working with one of these. But in addition to the difficulties already mentioned in using a long telephoto, you've now reached that point where the physical size of the lens becomes cumbersome. While some lens barrels are designed to be separated into two pieces for ease in carrying, you should plan on 20-24 inches in length for the standard glass designs, and 12-14 inches for the newer fluorite element lenses. In either case, you've got a good-sized package.

Filters can prove to be another headache. Many of these lenses require special screw-in filters ranging in size up to 95mm, and they are expensive—especially since they probably won't fit any other lens you might have. A few are designed to accept the insertion type mounted in special holders, while others allow the use of smaller screw-in filters (usually 30-49mm) on the rear of the lens. Incidentally, when using a filter with *any* long lens, you should always focus with the filter mounted in place, despite the difficulties you may encounter in viewing and focusing with certain ones like the deep reds, as the addition of a filter after the fact may cause a focus shift to take place.

To make their use easier, you'll find a pair of handy features built into some 600mm telephotos. As their focusing ring is often wider than the average hand, it takes a good grip and some effort to move it, but too much movement and you've overshot the mark. To prevent this and assist in more precise focusing faster, a screw-in handle similar in function to that used with

---

1-2. To show the dramatic reach of the 600mm, this Hollywood landmark was photographed on a sunny day from Los Angeles' Griffith Park with a 50mm and then a Vivitar Solid Cat. Note the flatter contrast of the 600mm shot, characteristic of telephotography in general and of mirror optics in particular.

telephoto photography/31

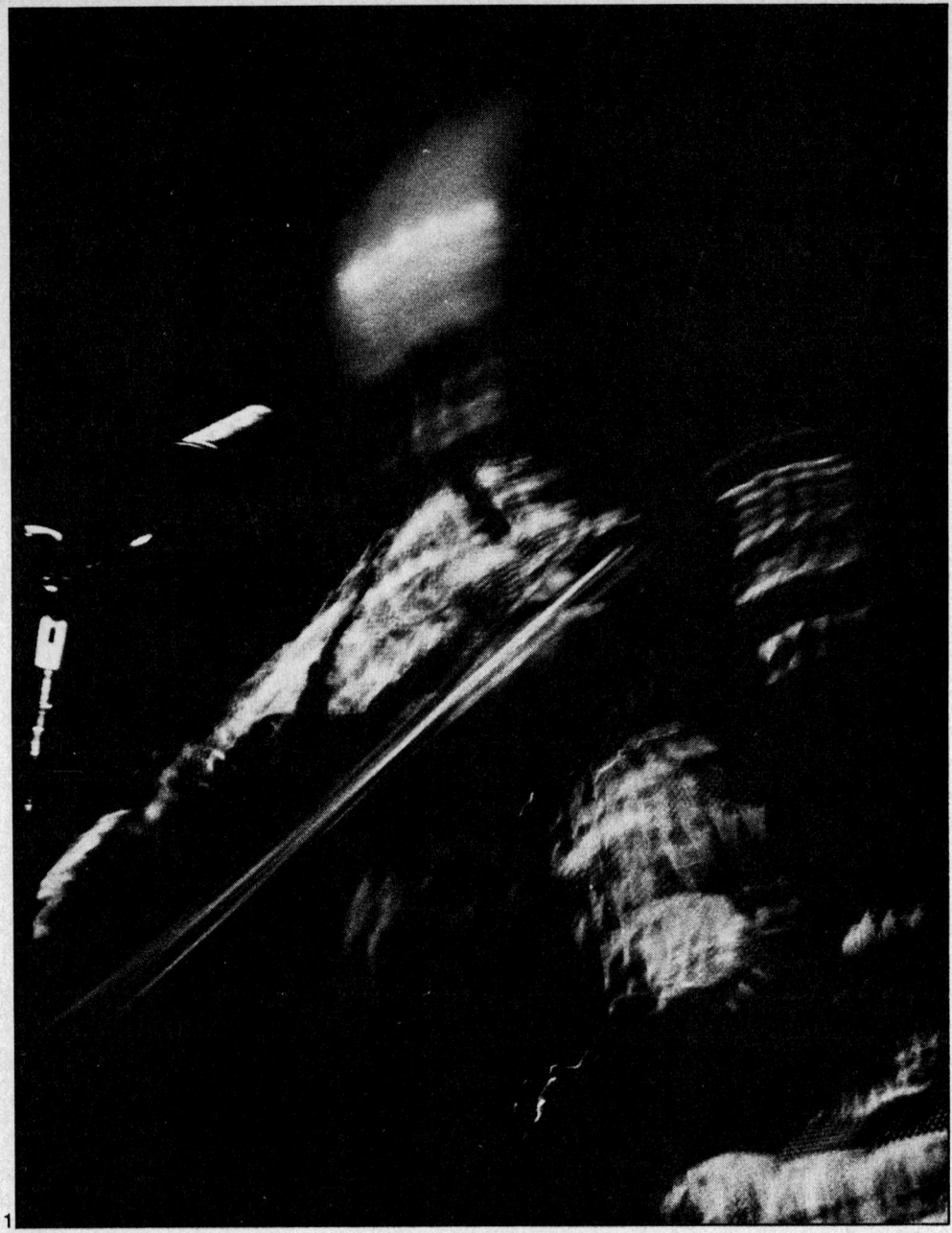

Hasselblads and other 6x6 SLR cameras is furnished. The leverage provided by this handle permits sure-fire focusing with only two fingers.

Looking into a viewfinder and sighting through a 20-inch optic to search for a moving object in a four-degree angular field of view hundreds of yards away can also be difficult at times; thus some manufacturers will mount a three-pronged sighting device on the front edge of the lens barrel and a single post at the rear of the barrel. Using these as you would an open rifle sight, you can move the camera and lens into position, framing the subject in the sighting device and then transferring your eye to the viewfinder to pick up the moving object. While it sounds awkward at first, once you catch onto using this arrangement, it'll prove invaluable for such work.

As you move beyond the 400mm, camera stability can become an increasingly frustrating experience. The ordinary tripod is unlikely to handle a 500-600mm if even a slight breeze is blowing, as some vibration is bound to occur. We'll discuss the selection and use of a proper tripod in a later chapter, but it's appropriate here to point out that even after mounting the camera and lens securely to your tripod, you shouldn't breathe a sigh of relief and forget the potential hazards of camera movement. Whenever possible, use the fastest shutter speed practical and trip the shutter with a cable release. If your camera has a mirror lock-up provision and the subject permits its use, lock the mirror up out of the way to prevent it from causing any vibration, and then release the shutter with the cable release or self-timer. With some tripods, it's possible to lend stability to the arrangement by simply bearing down on the lens just above the collar while making the exposure, but don't try this technique with lightweight tripods (those under six pounds) as it may aggravate the problem instead.

The upper end of this focal length range works beautifully for those occasions when you wish to fill the negative area with something that can barely be seen with the naked eye. Their 10-12X magnification factor will bring you up close to objects that are actually miles distant, as well as allowing you to work with creative cliches such as that oft-seen landscape silhouetted against the big red disk-like sun. These are certainly not lenses you'd carry around "just in case" you stumbled onto an appropriate subject, and only the very dedicated would lug one off on a vacation trip. Their relatively moderate speed (f/5.6-f/8) requires reasonably good lighting conditions in order to use a safe shutter speed, and should filtration of any sort be required, a fast emulsion is almost a necessity under most circumstances.

Putting these focal lengths to effective use for other than long-distance telephotography requires a good deal of imagination, forethought and advance planning on the part of the photographer; not only can

No matter how mouth-watering the prospect of such a lens seems to be, you're probably much wiser to regard the 400mm as the upper end of your telephoto equipment, at least until you've acquired the intermediate focal lengths between 50mm and 400mm, and have spent sufficient time working with them to maximize both your interest and enjoyment from the lenses. Once you've mastered their use and are looking for new aspects of telephotography to conquer, the 500-600mm then becomes a far more viable prospect.

Even at that, it's a focal length that will receive rather limited use by most amateurs, and you're perhaps better off exploring the extreme wide-angle lenses (if you haven't already done so), as you'll find far more uses for a 13-19mm super wide or even a full-frame fisheye optic than for this lower end of the super telephoto spectrum. But don't let my advice discourage you completely if you have the money and creative bent to put a 500-600mm to work—just make certain that you have thought the prospects over very carefully before buying a lens you may seldom put to use. □

1. This six-exposure effect of Pappy John Kreech in concert was photographed by Ron Berkenblitt with a 400mm using a motor drive while holding the rewind button in place.
2. Air shows are ideal for the telephoto. Ron Berkenblitt caught "The Human Fly" in action from the ground with a 400mm lens.
3. Crowds make it pretty difficult to get tight close-ups of performers at rock concerts, but Ron Berkenblitt captured Grace Slick from a considerable distance using his 400mm.
4. Don't overlook the possibilities of creative effects from telephoto shots. Ron Berkenblitt solarized this print to add an eerie feeling to the scenic forest shot.

the technical problems of size, camera movement and atmospheric interference be considerable, but creative use of their narrow angle of view makes the 500-600mm telephotos an unwise investment for the casual amateur, who may never use one sufficiently to justify the purchase.

800-2000mm

These are the telephoto optics of which most amateurs only dream—very few ever actually own one. The ultimate in telephotography, they will let you *identify* a person standing some 600-1200 feet away—a distance at which you can't even see your subject with the naked eye. Huge in power (16-40X magnification), large in size (averaging 30 inches long and weighing 10-15 pounds), and costly to buy (up to $9000 list), these "big guns" of the telephoto world are primarily specialized tools for professional sports coverage, space launches, wildlife, scientific, astronomical photography, or criminal investigation work.

About one-third of the lenses available in this supertelephoto category are of the mirror design, which brings their size, weight and cost down somewhat, but most are still exotic in more ways than you can count. Except for two 800mm optics, all have manual or preset diaphragms. While minimum focusing distance ranges from 16 feet for a 1250mm Honeywell Lumetar to 130 feet for the 1200mm Tele-Nikkor and Canon FL lenses, their speed is almost uniformly an f/8 aperture at the 800-1000mm focal lengths, and f/11 for the remainder.

Focusing such long lenses is a minor art, but the use of a rack-and-pinion device instead of the more traditional focusing ring does make the fine-tuning of your subject's focus considerably easier. The "system" optics, such as those offered by Nikon and Canon, make use of a front convertible design, in which the rear lens components, aperture diaphragm mechanism and focus adjustment device are all contained within a basic focusing unit that attaches to the camera body, and the various focal lengths are achieved by the use of different front components mounted in their own individual housing designed to fit into the focusing unit.

Hardly all-purpose lenses, the nature of the super-telephoto imposes severe limitations on when and how it can be used. While some of the mirror optics can be handled under many conditions with the use of a single tripod, the longer and heavier all-glass designs will generally require the use of two sturdy tripods to anchor the camera/lens arrangement securely at both front and rear. In addition, it may even be necessary to drape a sandbag or two over the lens to help minimize vibration, especially on a breezy day—and if the wind is gusting, forget it.

The use of a mirror lock-up, self-timer, cable release or any other method of tripping the shutter without *causing* vibration is of great importance, as in some cases just the operation of the shutter mechanism itself is sufficient to cause at least a minimal amount of vibration. Super-telephoto use is further restricted by atmospheric conditions to weather that is clear, cool and bright, as aerial haze and heat waves will prove pesky gremlins when you're reaching across a distance that's likely to extend miles from the camera to pick up a subject that you can't even see from your camera position.

When working with super-telephotos, some form of filtration will often be necessary. You should remember that the longer the focal length of the lens, the

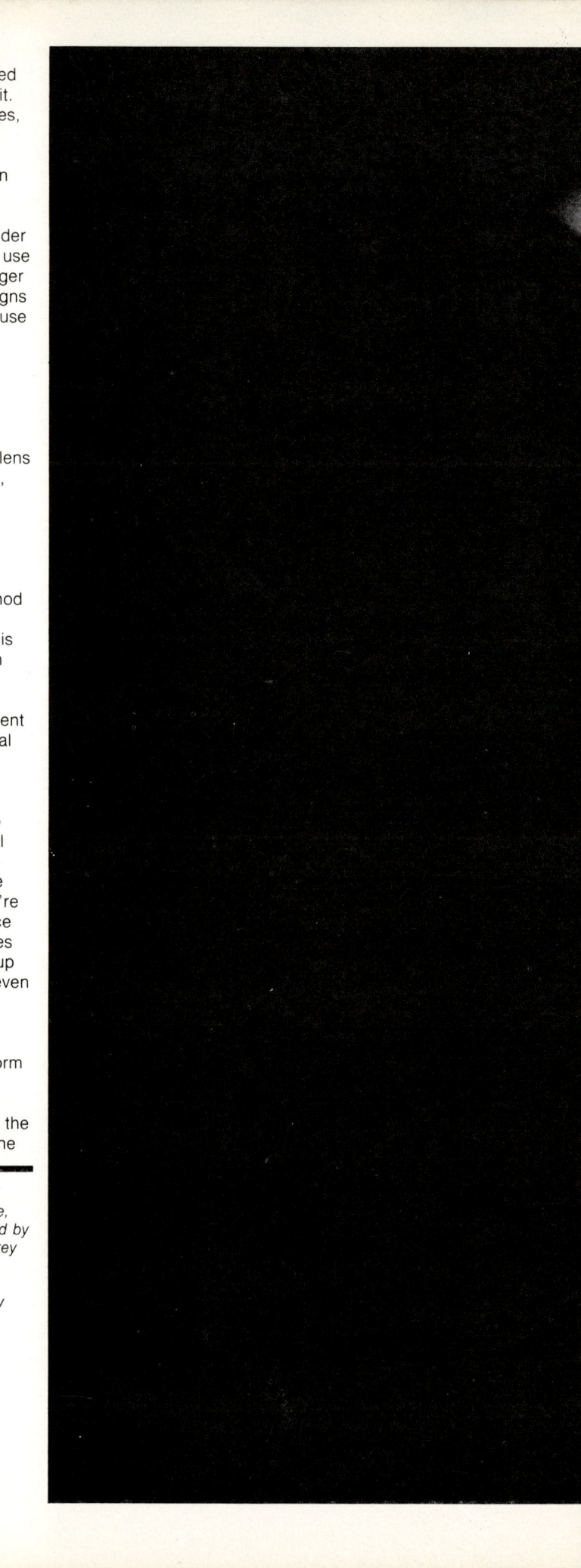

Silhouetted against the background of a solar eclipse, this jetliner was photographed by Wayne McGill and Mike Sankey for Celestron International to demonstrate the power of a 2000mm telephoto. (Courtesy Celestron International.)

higher the optical quality the filter used must be if you are to prevent unwanted distortion from affecting the image. The ideal placement for any filter is *between* the elements of the lens; the next best position is *behind* the lens. The super-teles all have provisions for either mounting standard size optical glass filters behind the lens, or the use of an insertion-type filter holder for working with the wide variety of gelatin filters available. Because filter gels (as they are known) are uniform in thickness, they possess excellent optical characteristics and are thus better suited than glass filters in cases where no reduction of image definition is desired.

Mirror optics in these focal lengths may also contain a built-in filter "wheel" or disc which can be revolved to bring the desired filter type into position in the light path. The filter wheels of less-expensive units contain fixed filters, while others permit their interchange to produce the exact filtration required for precise work in color. In either case, focusing must be done with the desired filter mounted in place if you are to prevent the possible occurrence of a shift in focus.

Because of the very long path which the light must travel from entering the lens until it strike the film, internal ghosts and reflections from lens flare may also cause degradation of the image. For this reason, it's important to have and use the proper lens shade when offered by the manufacturer.

Once the camera and super-telephoto have been tripod-mounted, maneuvering them can prove quite a task—but one which some manufacturers have made easier by fitting the lens barrel with a yoke arrangement that permits tilting the barrel up or down, or even revolving it horizontally to make any fine adjustments necessary to level the camera body, or

otherwise frame the subject as desired. This greatly simplifies the task when only one tripod is available; if two are used, only the one holding the camera body need be adjusted to correlate with the action of the yoke.

There are a number of relatively inexpensive super-telephotos available ($200-600 list), and once you discover that, you may be tempted in a moment of weakness to put one on your

1. One of the ultimates in compression, this maze of New York City street signs was taken by Edwin Hirsch for Celestron International using its 1250mm mirror optic at f/16. (Courtesy Celestron International.)
2. Sailboats leaving Marina del Rey, California are "stacked up" by Ron Berkenblitt with an 800mm. The degree of compression possible with a certain focal length depends upon both the subject distance from the camera, and the space relationship between the subject elements.
3. The normal flow of traffic captured with an 800mm does look impressive. Notice how restricted the range of sharpness is, even at f/11.
4. This plane had just left the airstrip and was starting to climb when caught with an 800mm telephoto—demonstrating apparent perspective shift between near and far objects photographed with a long telephoto.

charge account. But before taking that step, stop and ask yourself if such a purchase is really practical, or if you are not just indulging your fancies. Earlier, I mentioned that these were really specialized optics, but even those with a genuine use for such a lens

36/telephoto photography

will find only occasional use for it. For example, most nature photographers will work from blinds that are relatively close to their prey, relying upon lenses of more moderate focal length and greater speed, while sports photographers will go to any lengths to avoid using a super-telephoto unless it's absolutely necessary, such as at the Olympic games.

Although there's no doubt that the glamour of the super-telephoto lens and its ability to come up with clear, sharp pictures of an object the eye cannot even distinguish unaided do hold a fascination all their own, you'll do well to consider putting that extra money into one of the top-quality 400-600mm lenses with their own specially designed converters, such as the Minolta APO series, if such is offered to fit your camera. While the converter does have its own particular limitations, as we'll see in the chapter about converters, using one effectively is hardly as limiting as trying to work with an 800-1200mm lens, and you should consider that you'll have a top-notch prime lens in the shorter focal length which can be adapted on those rare occasions when you need the longer focal length lens.

One note of caution which should be heeded with lenses of *any* focal length, but which is most appropriate when working with the super telephoto: *Never try to view or photograph the sun without using a solar filter over the lens, as it can cause irreparable damage to your eyes.* This type of filter is coated with a neutral density substance that reduces the intensity of the sun's rays to approximately 1/100 of one percent at all wavelengths without affecting the effective aperture of your lens, and thus gives the necessary protection whenever you wish to use the solar disc as a background for those spectacular shots.

And so we've come to the end of a 1950mm journey through the world of the fixed focal length telephoto. By now, you should have a relatively clear idea of which ones will be of greatest use to you, some of their eccentricities, and how to best put them to work for you. Now it's time to change our pace and throw you a real curve ball by turning our attention to a consideration of that latest darling of the optical world—the modern zoom or variable focal length lens and its recent rival, the so-called macro or close-focusing zoom. □

telephoto color gallery

"Oil Wells at Sea." Ralph Abbott created this magnificent double exposure on High Speed Ektachrome Daylight rated at ASA 400. After photographing the moon with a 300mm and 3X converter (1/125 at f/16), he reexposed the basic scene with a 100mm for one second at f/4.

40/telephoto photography

1. Kodak Ektachrome Infrared exposed with a yellow filter and a 105mm gave John Chlumsky this striking balloon shot.
2. Wallpaper is wallpaper, until seen through a three-segment (triangular) prism attachment and an 85mm telephoto—then it becomes an abstraction.
3. Tramping through the Florida swamps, Michael Parrish captured these red winter berries with a 100mm.
4. Jeff Blackwell relied on a 300mm for impact, as well as bringing him within reach as these cyclists head into the home stretch.
5. Sometimes you simply cannot get close enough without the help of a telephoto. Steve Crecy composed this shot of a tram car with his 200mm.
6. Ken Moore found his 300mm and High Speed Ektachrome an ideal combination for this shot.

1. An 85mm gave Hal Stoelze this sunrise.
2. Ken Moore chose an oblique angle and a 300mm to compress these cemetary markers into an eerie composition.
3. Arthur Walker simulated one cause of the western drought by photographing the Denver skyline on Kodachrome X through a light orange filter, while holding a red filter in front of the lens to simulate the sun.
4. Michael Parrish found his 85-205mm zoom a useful companion while on a trip to the Republic of Panama. Its capacity for compositional control was put to good use, as in this picture, and saved carrying several individual focal length lenses on the trip.

telephoto photography/43

1. When you carry a telephoto, you automatically look for suitable subjects. Jeff Blackwell found one with his 200mm.
2. Steve Reed used a 1250mm Celestron mirror lens to provide this striking sunset as a background for this silhouette shot. (Courtesy Celestron International.)
3. Some assignments may require the use of a telephoto. The author found his 85mm very useful while doing a photo essay on pollution in Los Angeles city parks.

telephoto photography/45

telephoto zooms

When Petersen's *Interchangeable Lenses* first appeared late in 1974, there were some 87 zoom lenses available for use with 35mm format cameras. As this book is being written three years later, that number has increased by more than three dozen, with another 25 or so zoom optics introduced at Photokina '76 for marketing in 1977. This brings the total number of zoom lenses available to approximately 150 choices. Clearly, the continuous focal length lens has truly come of age. In those three intervening years, several new aspects have been added to accentuate the basic glamour of the zoom lens.

As *Interchangeable Lenses* went to press in 1974, the initial wide-angle/telephoto zooms had just made their appearance on the market, and they were heavy, bulky, very complex optically and quite expensive. Since that time, their size and weight have been considerably reduced, the optical complexity has been simplified, and the costs have been lowered accordingly. The telephoto and the wide-angle/telephoto zooms have been joined by the strictly wide-angle zoom, with focal length capability as short as 24-40mm. In addition, the large majority of current offerings have either been introduced as what is commonly called "macro" focusing, but should more appropriately be referred to as close-focusing zooms, or optically revised to include this feature. We'll discuss your basic needs and applications of the zoom lens at length here, and then deal with the close-focusing zooms in the following chapter.

HOW A ZOOM LENS WORKS

While the operation of a zoom lens was fully described in *Interchangeable Lenses*, the basic principle bears repeating for the benefit of those new to the hobby. Simply put, the zoom contains a *prime* or conventional camera lens positioned behind a variable power attachment whose focal point is afocal or at infinity. This prime lens remains stationary in use while the attachment moves to cause the change in focal length.

Since the prime lens is fixed at an infinity setting, it transmits the image provided by the afocal attachment to the film plane as one which originates at infinity, and thus is in sharp focus. Focusing is accomplished by moving the front portion of the afocal attachment in a manner similar to the front element focusing of lenses designed for use on the older folding cameras.

Zoom and focus functions may be controlled by separate rotating rings on the lens barrel, or the two functions may be combined in a single or rectilinear control which rotates for focusing and is drawn forward/backward on the lens barrel to control image size. Each has its own band of adherents, but most proponents of the "explosion/implosion" and

1-2. In addition to their compositional use, zoom lenses can be used creatively for effect. A quick zoom from the shortest to longest focal length (1) fills in the black background with glittering spots, while the slower zoom motion (2) creates a semihalo effect in which the model's features can be distinguished. (Ron Berkenblitt.)

other creative zoom effects prefer the single control ring.

WHAT CAN YOU DO WITH A ZOOM?

Without a doubt, the greatest benefit a zoom lens can offer the average photographer is a concise lesson in the fine points of composition and subject framing, because it allows instant and subtle changes in composition with none of the perspective problems inherent in changing your camera-to-subject distance. Using a zoom lens in this manner, you can study the relationship of subject-to-background, impact of the subject within the total negative area, and its effect in relation to any secondary objects that may be included.

While this can also be accomplished by the use of single focal length lenses, the beauty of a zoom remains unchallenged—it's all there at your fingertips, available instantly at the flick of a ring. For this reason, the zoom provides a quick and easy way of in-camera cropping, a real plus factor when you're shooting color slides. Unfortunately, few amateurs tend to use their zoom lens in this manner, and as a result, most would be better off working with individual focal lengths and learning to compose with them *before* moving on to zoom optics. But being human, we don't always do what's most beneficial, most practical or even most intelligent.

For the creative photographer, the zoom lens holds forth its unique ability to produce special effects on film. Utilizing the "explosion/implosion" technique requires that you choose both your subject and background with care. As it's necessary to maintain contrast in a picture that has no really sharp areas, there must be sufficient tonal differentiation between the two. When zooming from a short to a longer focal length, the image grows (explodes) in size during the exposure. If the background and subject are uniform in tone, it's obvious that no "explosion" is going to occur.

The camera must be mounted on a sturdy tripod if you wish to explore the potential of such optical effects. When you compose, leave sufficient room around the subject to accommodate the zoom effect and note the focal length setting. Zoom

the lens slowly to determine the degree of the effect and note the other focal length setting. You should use a slow film and a shutter speed no briefer than 1/8 second, depending upon the subject with which you're working and how accomplished you are at the technique.

The rest is simply a matter of practice. You release the shutter and zoom from one point to the other. Because you will be unable to tell what's happening by looking through the viewfinder, you should repeat the procedure several times to make sure you get an effect similar to that envisioned. Even experienced professionals who have worked with this technique often will shoot numerous exposures and are never absolutely certain of the effects captured until they see the processed film.

Working with this effect at night will give you a longer exposure time in which to manipulate the zoom control and it's possible to come up with some really spectacular shots of skylines, street scenes, carnivals, etc. For this reason, I'd suggest that you explore the technique after dark until you've got the feel of zooming and are confident in your ability to use the lens effectively.

ZOOM VS. SINGLE FOCAL LENGTHS

In an earlier chapter, I alluded to the fact that you should make a commitment at some point to acquire either individual focal length or zoom lenses. The sooner you can arrive at this decision, the less difficulty you'll find in choosing the proper lenses from among the ever-growing number available in both categories. You should have no qualms about the quality of current zoom lenses; with few exceptions, they are every bit as sharp as comparable single focal length optics for those uses to which most photographers will put them. This is not to say, however, that you won't occasionally find a lemon in either basket.

The major drawbacks to the use of most zoom lenses still remain their size, weight and speed, although a fair amount of progress in lens design and construction has alleviated many of the complaints in these areas—today's modern zooms often weigh less than the 2-4 individual optics they were meant to replace, and you have the residual benefits of all the in-between focal lengths. Still, if you require the use of an f/2.8

1-2. The speed and smoothness of the zooming motion during exposure determines the exact effect, as shown here. The staccato effect (1) indicates considerable hesitation during the zoom, while the more solid rays (2) show the use of continuous motion. Both received the same exposure in camera and under the enlarger, yet the windows in (2) are more clearly defined, another way of determining the type of motion used for the zoom.

3-5. Three different types of effects possible are shown here—all taken with a 75-260mm zoom. In (3), the focal length was changed only twice during the exposure to create a triple image; in (4), a continuous but not a smooth zoom motion was used; in (5), much of the four-second exposure was made at 75mm and when zoomed out to 260mm, the lens was thrown out of focus.

or faster maximum aperture at any given focal length, you'll find the zoom lens a handicap—except for a handful of very short zooms which cover some portion of the 35-100mm range, the usual maximum aperture remains something in the f/3.5 to f/4.5 bracket.

For those who are not averse to toting around several pounds of glass, brass and chrome on a day's outing, the magic appeal of the zoom lens becomes very difficult to resist. Imagine having a continuous focal length range from 24mm to 260mm at your fingertips, contained within a total of three lenses, or a 35mm to 300mm range in two lenses! It's almost too great a temptation to pass up, and that's why many who are beginners at the lens game now make a zoom their first accessory lens purchase—usually one in the 90-230mm or 85-205mm range.

Unless you can use a zoom lens to its maximum advantage, what's the point of having it? You're simply carrying around extra weight for nothing except that you know you have the capability, if and when it's needed. But at the same time, you've penalized yourself with a lens whose maximum aperture remains moderate in speed. As you can see, there are serious considerations both in favor of, and against the zoom lens. Which way you're going to go should be carefully thought out in advance or you may well end up with a lot of glass that you're not going to use.

When the first wide-angle/telephoto zooms came on the market, I bought one with the thought that it would replace my normal lens, my 35mm wide-angle and my 85mm telephoto. It was a fine idea in theory, but I grew so tired of carrying the camera with that heavy lens aboard that I went back to my 35mm for general work and carried the 85mm on my belt just in case. I haven't regretted disposing of the zoom, although I must confess that the concept still intrigues me.

HOW ABOUT A COMPROMISE?

With a little forethought and planning, it's possible to incorporate a zoom lens into your equipment without detracting from its value, or that of any individual focal length lenses you might already own. Exactly how you manage this will depend to a large extent upon the type of photography you most enjoy, and the nature of the subject matter with which you deal.

Those intrigued with photographing children would find a 45-100mm or 55-135mm zoom useful, but if wildlife photography is your primary interest, it's obvious that a wide-angle zoom is of little value to you, and a wide-angle/telephoto zoom would not offer much more. Yet, if you were to settle on a 100-300mm, the zoom could handle a good deal of your subject matter requirements with ease, while providing its unique compositional characteristics.

Some photographers prefer to work with a moderate zoom, such as a 35-70mm or 43-86mm, as their primary lens, supplementing its range with additional single focal length optics. Zooms which fall into this category are usually similar in size and weight to the camera's standard lens and at best, you're only sacrificing lens speed. Others reserve the zoom as their "special" lens and rely upon their individual lenses to handle the bulk of their photography, calling upon the zoom whenever extraordinary situations arise where its capabilities can best deal with the subject matter.

DO YOU REALLY NEED A ZOOM?

No, of course you don't—but those who believe everything they read in manufacturers' advertisements can easily be convinced that what they need is *three* zooms, not just one. In fact, beginners will do well to resist the siren call of the multiple focal length lens, as it has a distinct propensity to encourage them to stand away from their subject, when a far better viewpoint could be achieved by moving in on it.

It's a fact of life that the closer viewpoint invariably has more involvement with the subject, and as use of the zoom has no perceptible effect on perspective, a picture taken with the upper end of the zoom range will not produce the same effect which you could achieve by moving in closer. While the upper end of a zoom should be reserved for use primarily when it is difficult or otherwise impossible to move in closer, beginners tend to rely on its reach rather than change their viewpoint, a practice which limits their creative development severely.

Before you buy a zoom lens, there must be a definite reason or need for it, and one of the most convincing that manufacturers have yet come up with is the close-focusing capability incorporated in practically every zoom lens which has appeared in the past three to four years. Is it truly that useful a feature, can the close-focusing zoom really replace the macro lens, and is it a sufficient reason for purchasing a zoom lens? We'll look at that aspect next. □

close-focusing zooms

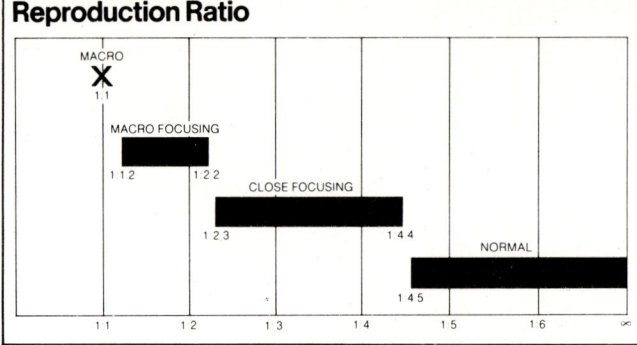

If you're confused about all the claims and counter-claims made for the close-focusing zoom lenses (often erroneously referred to as "macro" zooms), don't feel badly about your apparent inability to penetrate the various smoke screens and make an intelligent decision about them—it's really not that easy without certain information and guidelines which you'll seldom encounter in print. In this chapter, we intend to clarify a few points and give you the tools necessary to determine if you *really* need one, and if so, how to pick the one best suited for you.

To begin with, let's destroy the "macro" myth which manufacturers have perpetuated from the time Kilfitt first brought forth the term to describe its close-focusing Macro-Kilar lenses in the 1950s. Correctly defined, macro photography involves an image size on the film *equal to or larger than* the object being photographed—expressed mathematically as a *reproduction ratio* of 1:1 or a *magnification ratio* of 1X, but sometimes also called "life-size."

Kilfitt's competition saw fit to apply the term "macro" in describing their own close-focusing lenses, but as the industry made the switch to automatic diaphragm, the resulting mechanical coupling problems caused the manufacturers to reduce the reproduction ratio of their lenses to 1:2 or even 1:3, which means that the maximum image size is one-half or one-third that of the object being photographed. Yet by providing an extension tube with the lens to restore its reproduction ratio to 1:1, the use of the term "macro" was retained. This situation remained fairly stable for over a decade, until zoom lens designers got into the act.

Nonzoom lenses are usually focused by moving the entire optical assembly as a single unit. But to retain sharp focus while changing the focal length in a zoom lens, it is necessary to resort to front-element focusing—a forward/backward motion of the front part (one or more elements) of the afocal attachment. Unfortunately, this presents certain optical limitations which prohibit most zoom lenses from focusing closer than 4-6 feet, depending upon their particular design and focal length range.

Many users objected, feeling this lack of closer focusing ability to be one of the limitations of zoom optics. After all, a 55-135mm zoom which focuses to five feet is equal to most 135mm lenses (which also focus to five feet) when used at its longer focal length, but the 55mm end that only focuses to five feet is a distinct disadvantage when compared to the camera's

1. Vivitar has attempted to introduce order into the macro/close-focusing zoom controversy by labeling its lenses according to the possible reproduction ratio obtainable. Whether other manufacturers will follow suit remains to be seen, but its attempt to define what's what can be helpful to potential purchasers confused by close-focusing claims.
2. Hanging a stained glass ornament in front of a rain-streaked window, John Guarente used the Vivitar 70-210mm Series 1, which permits close-ups only at the 210mm focal length.

normal lens, which can usually be focused to 18-24 inches. It was to this problem that zoom lens designers began to address themselves, and by late 1973, various solutions to the problem, most of which involved an alteration in the position of some of the optical components, began to appear on the market. These were often described in print as having "macro" focusing capability.

As different designs approached the problem of close-focusing from different aspects, we now have zoom lenses displaying a variety of close-focusing abilities—in other words, close-focusing zooms of the same focal length range may not be equal in their close-focusing ability. When set in the so-called "macro" mode, some which use a rearrangement of their elements are functional only at one focal length (usually their maximum) and thus cannot be used for close-ups at any other zoom setting. Others of this type may provide close-focusing at any focal length setting. A number of the close-focusing zooms do not use rearrangement of the elements, but rely instead upon a combination of front-element focusing and the use of a short rear extension on the lens to focus to a closer point than is possible with just front-element focusing. This permits the use of all focal lengths in the close-up mode, but this type also delivers its greatest magnification or reproduction ratio at its shortest focal length. Still another variation uses the twin concept of front-element focusing and the extension, but as the zoom control device is uncoupled from the optical train when used to actuate the extension, close-focusing is possible only at the shortest focal length.

And there you have the problem in a nutshell—with so many design variations available, and so many differences existing in the reproduction ratio they provide, which may deliver a maximum image magnification ranging from 1:1.3 to 1:6—how do you make the right choice? Of course, the first question you should ask yourself is, "Do I really need a close-focusing zoom lens?" to which the answer may well be a resounding NO. Look at the problem this way—a standard 55mm lens which

focuses to 18 inches will deliver a reproduction ratio of approximately 1:5 without the use of any accessories. If the close-focusing zooms in which you've expressed an interest cannot do better than a 1:5 reproduction ratio at their close-up setting, why buy one?

Listening to a salesman across the counter, you can be overwhelmed by hearing that while a certain zoom lens normally focuses to 8½ feet, setting it in the close-up or "macro" mode will let you photograph your subject from a mere 24 inches away, or that another comparable zoom which focuses to six feet under normal conditions can be used at 12½ inches in its close-up setting.

Such impressive statistics are usually sufficient to clinch the sale right on the spot, but if you bring out the paper and pencil to do a little math first, you'll discover that *both* zooms provide a maximum image magnification or reproduction ratio of only 1:4! Which brings us to our first criterion of judgment—forget the close-focusing claims and consider only the magnification or reproduction ratio of the zoom lens in question. Incidentally, here's another little tidbit of which you should be aware—if the close-focusing feature of the lens can be used at all focal lengths, the reproduction ratio will not be the same at the longest focal length as at the shortest. If the lens gives you a 1:4 ratio at the shortest focal length, the ratio at the other end of the zoom is more likely to be in the neighborhood of 1:5.5 or

1:6, depending upon the focal length range.

O.K., so let's suppose that you've found a close-focusing zoom lens which has a substantial enough reproduction ratio to be of interest to you. Your friendly salesman is likely to assure you as part of his sales pitch that this zoom will equal in quality most of the standard "macro" lenses, and outperform many of the others—is he right?

Not exactly—remember that virtually every zoom lens manufactured suffers to some extent from a certain amount of barrel distortion at one end of the focal length range, and from pincushion distortion at the other end. Now, logic tells us that if this is so, there must be some point along the focal length range where barrel distortion turns into pincushion distortion and vice versa. If you can locate that exact focal length, you'll have the point at which linear distortion is at a minimum in your particular lens. But what if *your* lens has close-focusing capability only at the long or short end of the focal length range?

What we've just discovered is our second criterion of judgment—that the close-focusing zooms can vary considerably, both in their capability to do flat copy work of the exact size you may want, and to do it without some degree of distortion, which may well be objectionable. You should not be surprised to learn that generally speaking, the greater the magnification ratio, the less sharp the reproduction you'll obtain from flat objects, as true flatness of field (edge-to-edge sharpness) is more difficult to achieve at greater magnification levels.

Yet, most of these lenses will do an adequate job (and some do very well) when working in the close-up mode with three-dimensional objects, especially when they can be stopped down to f/8 or f/11. As such subjects usually do not require edge-to-edge sharpness, you probably won't even notice the slight amount of curvature of field, especially if you can work at that optimum focal length position where linear distortion is held down as much as possible. In fact, with some subjects, such as insects in their natural habitat, curvature of field at the edges will serve much the same purpose as deliberately throwing the background out of focus.

Now you can understand why it's so important to thoroughly analyze your needs for a close-focusing zoom, as well as determining which one will best do the job you envision for it. Just because the salesman's demonstration is impressive over the counter, you should not lay out $200-700 for such a lens without fully understanding exactly what it will and won't do. This can be an open invitation to a rude awakening when you get home with it and finally have the time to put your new purchase through its paces, only to discover that it really doesn't do what you thought it would.

Even studying those comparison charts to try and psych out the various options you have in mind is no real substitute for our third criterion—take your camera body to the store with you, know exactly what you expect of the lens in advance and insist on a demonstration. Then politely thank the salesman, go home and *think* about it some more, especially if you already own a zoom lens, but one without the close-focusing feature.

For the most part, the close-focusing zoom lenses with much to be commended, especially at this stage in the state of the art which brought it about. But at the same time, there's no doubt that the advantages and capabilities have been blown out of proportion by advertising copywriters and camera store salesmen. If you already own a satisfactory zoom lens, there's no reason to succumb to that itch to trade it for the newest, as the newest may not necessarily be the best for your purposes. And if you've already learned your lesson the hard way, you have my sympathy, as I learned mine that way too! □

1-2. As an all-around utility lens, the close-focusing zoom does offer certain advantages, especially if you simply cannot come physically closer to your subject. Photographed with an 80-200mm Prinz zoom set at its closest point of focus for both the 80mm (1) and 200mm (2) focal lengths, this 1¾-inch trinket shows the difference in size obtainable with a standard zoom. 3-4. Switching the 80-200mm into its close-focusing mode for a 1:4 reproduction ratio, the same trinket was then photographed at its closest point of focus for both the 80mm (3) and 200mm (4) settings. 5-6. For comparison, here's the image size obtainable with a 105mm macro lens at its nearest point of focus and set for reproduction ratios of 1:4 (5) and 1:2 (6). 7. By moving his 70-210mm Vivitar Series 1 slightly closer to the subject than its nearest point of close focusing, John Guarente combined the resulting softness with Kodak 2475 Recording Film for this delicate interpretation of a rose.

catadioptric lenses

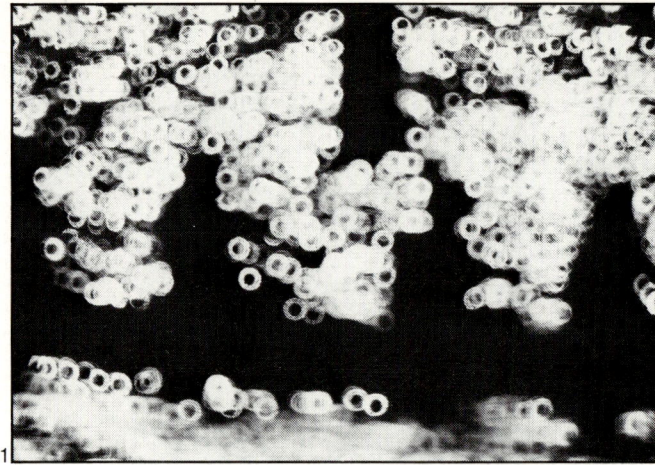

Some years ago, the *catadioptric* or mirror lens enjoyed a reasonable amount of popularity—manufacturers made lots of them and many were sold under a great variety of brand names other than that of their manufacturer. Unfortunately, their liabilities were as pronounced as their assets, and with a few exceptions mirror optics virtually disappeared from the scene only to return again recently with increased vigor, and in numbers which guarantee that they'll be around for a long stay this time.

So what's a mirror lens, you ask? As you know, in the conventional long focus or refracting telescope design, light rays which enter the lens's front element are transmitted to the film plane in a straight line. This results not only in a long focal length, but also in a long physical length, and one of considerable weight. But in the catadioptric design, the light rays that enter the front of the lens are folded back and forth several times via a mirror optical system utilizing the principle of the reflecting telescope. Folding of the light path in this manner results in a short physical length of the lens barrel, reducing the travel of its front relative to the film plane to greatly increase the sharpness of hand-held photographs.

However, mirror optics do possess several disadvantages:

1—Their manufacture is very tricky, as arrangement of the mirrored surfaces must be very precise. Such a system is prone to damage from an impact which would not affect a refracting design, but can easily cause misalignment of the mirror components.

2—Optical alignment of the components has been known to vary according to changes in atmospheric pressure or temperature.

3—The hollow center of the light cone may result in a hot spot (illumination falloff toward the corners) and a lack of contrast in some designs.

4—As it is not possible to incorporate a diaphragm in the catadioptric design, the lens must be used at a constant, fixed f-stop.

5—Because of its reflecting design, the mirror lens will generally transmit between two-thirds to one full f-stop *less* light to the film plane than its rated speed. This factor is also dependent upon design, as different types of mirrored surfaces transmit light with varying degrees of efficiency.

Yet for each disadvantage,

1. Out-of-focus highlights turn into ring-shaped donuts, resulting in fantastic effects. Photographing a college rowing team in competition, Ron Berkenblitt threw his subjects slightly out of focus with a 1000mm Reflex-Nikkor, blending them into the circular highlights—imagine this in color! 2. Glenn Cooper caught Tom Griffen of the San Diego Padres in action from the dugout at Dodger Stadium with a 500mm mirror optic, demonstrating that it has practical uses too even if the spectators did turn into tiny donuts.

there's an equally important advantage:

1—Mirror optics are extremely small and lightweight when compared to conventional long focus lenses of the same focal length. This reduction of size and weight makes it possible to hand-hold many 500mm and 750mm mirror lenses without undue camera movement.

2—Mirror lenses can be focused to a near point usually one-half to one-third of the distance at which conventional designs can be focused.

3—Secondary color aberrations found in conventional glass lenses are absent from the mirror designs.

4—The mirror lens turns out-of-focus highlights into ring-shaped donuts, producing spectacular special effects.

5—Exposure control can be manipulated by using a neutral density filter. This allows retention of the shorter depth-of-field factor for creative purposes.

The recent proliferation of mirror lenses seems to be part and parcel of the increasing popularity of long focal length lenses, and seeing a market that clearly required innovation if it were to grow, several manufacturers plunged ahead with new designs. Probably the most important, because of the impetus as well as the impact it had on other manufacturers, Vivitar announced three new Solid Catadioptric lenses at Photokina in 1974—a 600mm f/8, an 800 f/11 and a 1200 f/11—and showed a prototype of a 600-900mm Solid Catadioptric f/12 zoom at Photokina in 1976.

Designed in conjunction with the American optical firm of Perkin-Elmer Corporation, the *Solid Cat*, as it's known, incorporates space-age technology to create a major break-through in telephoto lens design. Unlike other mirror optics, the Cat is constructed of two pieces of identical optical material assembled together. Using a number of such spherically shaped lens elements cemented together to form what amounts to a single element, the solid glass construction results in an incredibly compact (3 5/16-inch long), three-pound lens which has a very high resistance to damage by shock. It also has the ability to maintain precise optical alignment despite extremes in temperature. Flare is virtually nonexistent because of the baffling used, and antireflective coating of the elements practically eliminates the hot spot common to previous catadioptric designs.

The next most influential design to appear in the mirror lens field has to be the new 700mm f/8 Questar—a mirror optic

54/telephoto photography

Neither lens is inexpensive—the Cat lists for $822 and the Questar at $995—but both offer substantial design improvements over comparable optics, whether of the conventional refracting or mirror type, and will certainly be in demand by those who want or need the best. While it's true that the average photographer may never own a Solid Cat or a Questar, both lenses are still important additions to the field of mirror lenses and telephotography in that they've provided the competitive push to spur other manufacturers in their thinking.

As an example, Minolta has quietly expanded its mirror lens offerings to four different focal lengths with its recent addition to the line of the smallest and lightest 500mm yet seen. Its f/8 RF Rokkor-X measures 3 5/16 inches in diameter, is 3⅞ inches in length and weighs a mere 23¾ ounces. While its optical design is not a startling departure from the usual approach to mirror optics, it is clearly a refinement, using the latest in technology that is bound to influence other manufacturers.

To this point, I've discussed mirror lenses that you probably can't afford yet, so let's look at the rest of the field. Current offerings range from a 150mm Nye Super Tele to a 3900mm Celestron, but the majority available are 500mm. These can cost anywhere from $149 to $22,450—list price, of course. Obviously, the great majority of us are more interested in the $149 model—is it worth the money, and if it is, why the great disparity in price?

Actually, there are two different designs available in this approximate price range, and both are discounted to a more reasonable price. Each is offered under various trade names, but you can spot them by their exterior design, as nothing has been changed except the name and the price. The Caspeco, Cambron, Hanimex, Prinz and Samigon all come from

specifically designed for photographic use by the manufacturers of Questar telescopes. Previous Questar models have long been adapted for photography, but this newest is the first Questar destined to have a significant impact on general photography.

Weighing in at about four pounds, the nine-inch lens has a field that's virtually flat with no linear distortion visible, almost even illumination from center to edge with superb definition for such a lens, and a near point of focus at 10 feet with an image magnification of 1:4. For those who wish to put it to the same dual use accorded other Questars in the past, a top-quality eyepiece is available to transform it into a telescope. Like the Solid Cat, the new Questar mounts to almost any SLR by means of a T-adapter.

telephoto photography/55

the same Japanese factory. Measuring 7½ inches in length and four inches in diameter, this mirror lens weighs three pounds, seven ounces, has a rated aperture of f/8 and contains a revolving neutral density filter wheel to offer exposure capability equivalent to f/11 and f/16 apertures. A screw-in lens hood is furnished, and any 77mm filters can be used on the front of the lens.

With a closest marked focusing distance of 10 feet, its 1:5 image magnification ratio puts this lens right in the ball game. What kind of pictures will it take? Under most circumstances, more than adequate ones. While its contrast is a bit on the low side and there is a moderate hot spot, neither defect should be noticeable with average subjects unless you have a perfectly plain background such as a blue sky occupying much of the picture area. Although it's not the sharpest biting optic of its kind on the market, much of whatever softness you might note in your pictures can probably be traced to a problem in focusing due to the lower contrast. It is worth noting, however, that there seem to be greater variations between samples of mirror lenses than those of refracting telephoto designs.

The other modestly priced 500mm mirror lens is the f/8 Sigma XQ, also sold by Spiratone as its Ultratel. This has a smaller and weaker main mirror, but uses extra lenses for better correction, which helps explain the 8⅝-inch length, 3 5/16-inch diameter and two-pound, 3½-ounce weight. The lens hood is a retractable one, but 77mm filters can also be used at the front of the lens. Closest marked focusing

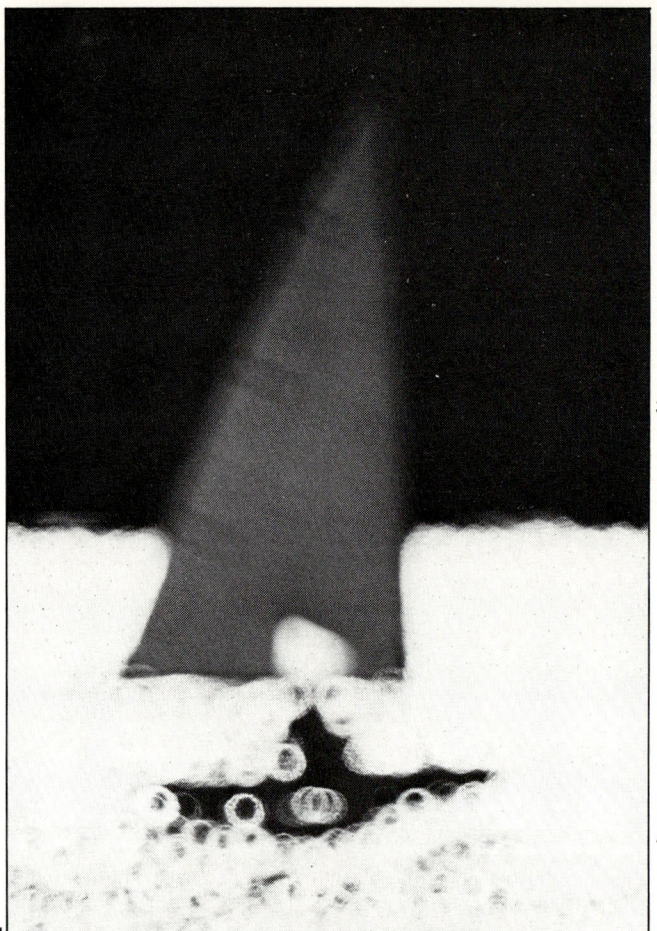

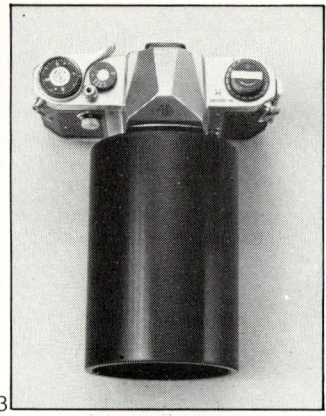

1. Another special effect by Ron Berkenblitt, the sailboat becomes an unworldly apparition when photographed with the 1000mm Reflex-Nikkor and a polarizer.
2. For super donuts (and spectacular effects in color), Ron Berkenblitt positioned his subject at the minimum focusing distance of his 1000mm Reflex-Nikkor with the sun and sea behind, turning the subject into a silhouette and the ocean into a wild display of multicolored rings.
3. The Lyman Alpha I by Nye Optical (Spring Valley, California 92077) is a relatively inexpensive 200mm f/2.8 (as mirror lenses go), shown here attached to a Pentax SLR.
4. Nye Optical offers a large variety of mirror optics using the radial vane design. This is a 150mm f/1.4 mirror lens focusing to nine inches!

distance is 13 feet, with a 1:7 image ratio. Overall contrast is better in this lens, making it somewhat easier to focus. Sharpness is also slightly better on a test bench, but I doubt very much that you would be able to tell the difference if this lens and one of the other design were both tripod-mounted and used to photograph the same subject under identical conditions.

Speaking of tripods, don't let them fool you about hand-holding the lower-priced mirror lenses. You *can* do it, of course, but there's definitely a difference in image sharpness between lenses in this price bracket and those costing several hundreds or thousands of dollars more. While the lighter Sigma XQ is easier to hold than its competitor, both will benefit from all the help you can give them—tripod, cable release, mirror lock-up, fast shutter speed, etc.

You should also be aware that both designs will focus past infinity—this is provided to compensate for different camera adapters, as well as any slight focus changes in the optics caused by extreme changes in temperature. For this reason, you must focus accurately on a subject of infinity, instead of simply setting the focusing ring to its stop.

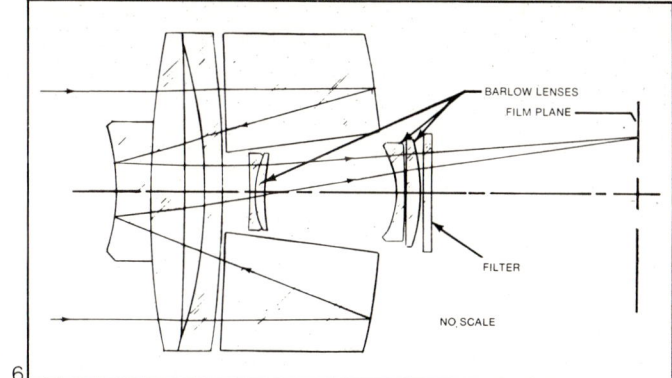

5. A chief virtue of the mirror lens is its compact size compared to the standard refracting telephoto design. This is the Vivitar 600mm Solid Cat, the latest in catadioptric design.
6. The Vivitar Solid Cat uses two spherically shaped elements cemented together to form one. This "single" element results in a compact, lightweight, shock-resistant lens without the flare and hot spot common to other mirror designs.

What can you use a mirror lens for? Virtually any photographic situation calling for a lens of its focal length—and the portability of a mirror optic is a big plus over that of a comparable focal length of the refracting design. You might feel handicapped somewhat by the slight loss of light transmitted to the film, but with the recent appearance of faster color emulsions, or a bit of push-processing for black-and-white if necessary, this should not pose an insurmountable problem.

But best of all, those who enjoy working with special effects will delight at the possibilities inherent in those donut-shaped, out-of-focus highlights, especially when working with color film and/or special filtration. For more information on applying this technique, see the *Special Effects* volume of Petersen's How-To PhotoGraphic Library. From where I stand, owning a mirror optic is like having two lenses in one—you have the same shallow depth-of-field and the space compression factors common to all long focal length lenses, and the unique creative potential offered by the reflecting telescope design. Treat the lens with the same care that you'd give any other piece of precision equipment and it'll deliver the same fine pictures you expect from it as well. □

press and view camera telephotos

Thus far, we've discussed telephotography primarily with the 35mm camera user in mind, but with the recent revival of interest in, and use of the view camera, it would not be proper to completely ignore those readers who have found a new interest in photography via the large-format negative. While a vast number of lenses have been manufactured over the years for press/view camera use, most are no longer obtainable new, because the cost of producing such optics and the relatively limited demand in recent years has driven many companies to discontinue production. But you still have a wide choice, as the range and variety of used lenses far exceeds that available for any other format.

All you have to do is locate the one you want. The used-lens section of most large camera shops is generally filled with press/view camera lenses of varying focal lengths, many of which can still be obtained at a reasonable price, although the larger dealers have caught onto the trend and prices are now rising accordingly. Those few manufacturers who still offer new press/view optics can supply a complete selection of excellent lenses, but today's prices reflect both the quality of current lens design, and the inflationary spiral of the past few years. New view camera lenses of good quality at a reasonable price are almost a thing of the past.

If you're not familiar with the requirements of the large-format camera, you've probably just entered the world of instant confusion, especially when dealing with "normal" view camera lenses. Unlike hand camera types, it's the "circle of coverage" or covering power of a particular lens that governs its use.

As view camera lenses are moved off-axis whenever camera movements are utilized, they are generally of a focal length somewhat longer than the diagonal of the negative. This is necessary to assure that the field of coverage is sufficient to accommodate the required camera swing, tilt, rise or fall, with even illumination and definition from one corner of the negative to the other.

The minimum image circle diameter required to adequately cover the negative's diagonal with a 4x5 view camera is 161mm; with a 5x7, 219mm; and with an 8x10, 323mm. Yet for those types of photography where camera movements will not be made, it's possible to use shorter focal length lenses because with most, the circle of coverage expands as the aperture is

stopped down. Thus, a given lens will cover more at f/22 than at f/8. This is also true when the lens is used for close-up photography—as the distance increases between its optical center and the film plane, so does the circle of coverage increase.

While a 150-165mm lens will serve as a general or "normal" focal length for most work with a 4x5 view camera where camera movements will be moderate, if used at all, the 210-240mm range (equivalent to a 63-72mm focal length for 35mm cameras) is preferred by many professionals for everything from product illustration and portraiture to subjects that require maximum perspective correction with full camera

1. Photographed by Ron Berkenblitt with a 4x5 Calumet view camera and 210mm Symmar lens, this panoramic view of the UCLA rowing team was achieved by printing only the top third of the 4x5 negative. 2-4. This sequence demonstrates the dramatic increase in image size which the 300mm (3) and 360mm (4) provide over the 210mm (2) used as a normal lens on a 4x5 view. These three lenses are equivalent to using a 63mm, 90mm and 110mm with the 35mm format. (Ron Berkenblitt.)

space (or flattening of the perspective) will move into the 500mm range, which can be roughly equated with a 150mm telephoto for 35mm cameras.

Telephoto photography with press/view cameras is limited only by the maximum length or draw of the camera's bellows. A nine-inch bellows extension will permit the use of lenses up to approximately 14-inch focal lengths, while a 13-inch bellows will accommodate up to about 18 inches, etc. If the lens in question is a true telephoto design with a shorter back focus than the rated focal length, considerably longer effective focal lengths can be used. As some of the older 4x5 cameras such as the Plaubel Pro 4x5 had a 39-inch bellows draw, they were able to accept 36-42-inch telephoto lenses, which proved the equivalent of a 280-300mm telephoto on a 35mm camera. Of course, view camera lenses with focal lengths like these are mammoth in size, weighing some 15-18 pounds and requiring that special supports be fitted to the camera, as well as mounting the lens on a special tripod, but think of the image they would deliver—and the quality!

Don't expect to find the large aperture lenses that other cameras use available in press/view focal lengths—they aren't available and really aren't necessary. Sharp definition is what you're looking for, and to get it in most cases, you'll stop the lens down to f/32 or even f/45. As such lenses are very highly corrected and involve the use of large glass surfaces, a maximum aperture of f/4.5 is considered a very fast lens; you'll find that f/5.6 or f/6.3 is a more common maximum aperture, and many of the longer focal length lenses will be restricted to a speed of f/8 or f/11.

Now, how do you go about locating a good used view camera lens suitable for telephoto work? Start searching through local photo stores. When you find one of interest, you should

fit it to your camera body and work from that point. Those who are relatively new to photography may not recognize the brand names that once represented an ultimate level of quality in such optics; such readers will not be led astray with any of the following brand/trade names: Bausch & Lomb, Dallmeyer, Goerz Apochromat Artar or Dagor, Graflex Tele-Optar, Gundlach Turner-Reich Convertible, Kodak Commercial Ektar, Ilex New Paragon, Wollensak Raptar Tele or Zeiss Tessar.

Generally speaking, stick with post-World War II designs that have been coated. Check the surface of the lens by reflected light for a fine network of tiny scratches, which would indicate that its former owner spent more time polishing the front element than taking pictures. Don't be too fussy about the appearance of the mount's finish, but do keep an eye out for any nicks or dents which might indicate that the lens had been dropped, as this may have affected its centering. Look at a white light source through the lens and if you notice any yellowish cast, it most likely indicates that the cement used between the elements has discolored and is decomposing. White fernlike designs seen between the elements will mean an unchecked fungus growth. If you're fortunate enough to find tiny bubbles in the glass, you have a lens that bears what was once considered as the ultimate hallmark of quality; don't be put off by it. Whatever defects you find can all be corrected, but you might as well pass the lens by and look for another, since the cost of renovating it will often exceed the price of a new one. □

movements. For portraiture without distortion and a moderate increase in image magnification, use of a 254-305mm lens (equivalent to an 85-90mm for 35mm cameras) is recommended as a good compromise focal length, but those interested in a visible compression of

auxiliary telephoto devices

Up to this point, we've discussed only prime lenses—those optics which are complete and integral to themselves, replacing the camera's normal lens for use. Common sense will tell you that such lenses produce the highest image quality obtainable, and that any add-on attachment will of necessity introduce a certain amount of image degradation, by introducing its own optical aberrations and deficiencies into the optical path.

But millions of Americans own and enjoy telescopes, and I'm certain that if you're one of them, you've often eyed the scope and wondered about using it with your SLR. It is possible and if done correctly, will produce results you probably won't believe. While it's preferable to use a scope such as the Bushnell Spacemaster described shortly, in which the camera lens is removed and the image is formed only by the telescope's objective, you can use any telescope in the following manner:

1—Mount the scope on a sturdy tripod and position the camera on another tripod behind it, with the camera lens as close to the telescope eyepiece as possible. The use of a wide-angle lens or one in which the front element is recessed will result in some vignetting at the negative corners.

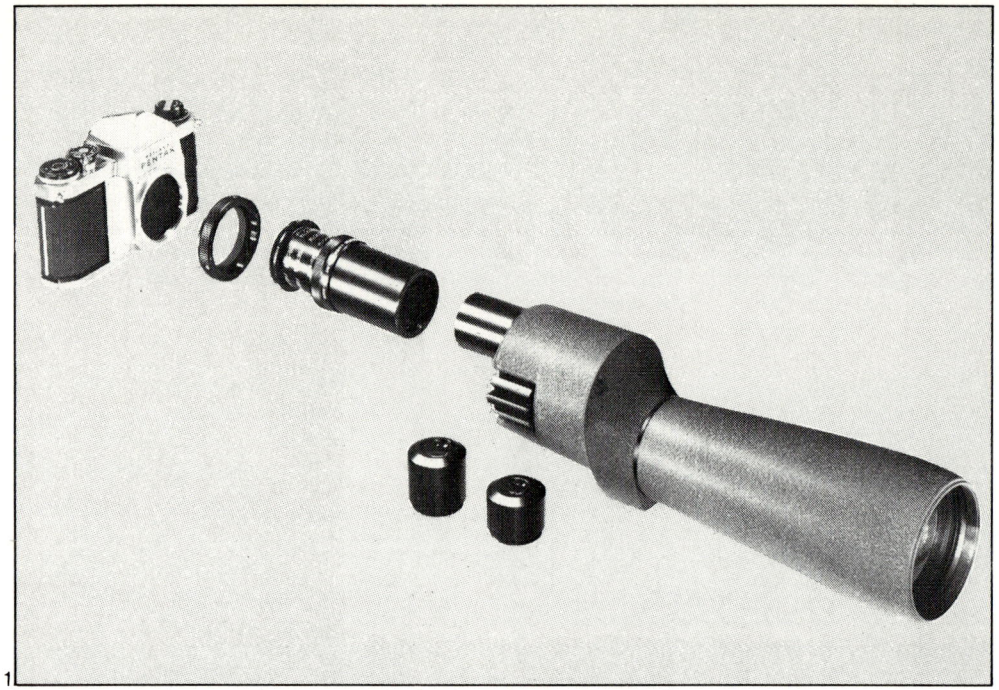

2—Leave the camera's diaphragm wide open, as it has no bearing on the effective aperture which results from such a combination. Your effective aperture will be predetermined by the magnification of the telescope used.

3—If you wish to calculate the effective aperture, the formula is:

$$f = \frac{FP}{D}$$

F = focal length of the camera lens.
P = the telescope power.
D = diameter of the objective in mm.

This is really necessary only if you're curious, or use

1. Bushnell's Spacemaster telescope is designed for double duty, coupling with popular SLR cameras to provide focal lengths from 750mm to 3000mm.
2. The Quantaray Zoom Fotocular is both small and lightweight, yet provides a magnification range equal to 400/1000mm when used with a 50mm lens.
3. Photographed with a 50mm lens on a 35mm SLR, the water tower shown in the circled area is barely visible.
4. But add a Quantaray Zoom Fotocular and adjust for the 1000mm range—here it is. Slight vignetting is normal, as is the loss of contrast.

a camera body without a built-in metering system.

4—Focus the camera lens on infinity, as focusing will be done with the telescope.

5—Use a cable release and follow the other suggestions I've passed along for long-range photography, as the effects of aerial haze, air turbulence, camera movement, etc. apply equally to the use of a telescope.

Those who have a standard Bushnell Spacemaster (not the 45-degree or zoom model) can turn it into a super telephoto with focal lengths ranging from 750mm to 3000mm, depending upon the interchangeable eyepiece used. The camera lens is replaced by a camera body adapter to which a variable camera mount is attached, providing proper alignment and rigidity automatically. This mount is engraved with focal lengths and f-stop values for a quick selection of telephoto effects. Three interchangeable eyepieces have been made available:

1—15X—provides 750 to 1500mm telephoto effect (magnification from 15 to 30 power).

2—20X—provides 1500 to 2160mm telephoto effect (magnification from 30 to 43 power).

3—25X—provides 2160 to 3000mm telephoto effect

3

4

(magnification from 43 to 60 power).

Those who do not own a Spacemaster or other telescope, but are interested in telephotgraphy on a limited budget, might try a zoom monocular offered by Ritz Camera, 11710 Baltimore Avenue, Beltsville, Maryland 20705 as the Quantaray Zoom Fotocular. Considering the capability which it offers, this 16-ounce, screw-on auxiliary lens should prove a fascinating addition to your camera, adding only seven inches to the front of your normal lens at an approximate cost of $7 per inch. Monoculars (half a binocular) have been around for many years now, and previous attempts to use them for telephotography have produced so-so results. But a seven-element, five-group varifocal monocular covering an 8X to 20X magnification range (equivalent to 400-1000mm) is something different.

To use the Fotocular, you screw it into the camera's normal lens via the adapter provided and mount the whole affair on a tripod. After setting the camera lens focus at infinity, open the diaphragm and reach to the front of the monocular, where you'll find a focal length selector knob in an arc-shaped slot calibrated between 8X and 20X. Pick your magnification and then turn the knurled focusing ring at the front of the unit. Simple enough? The degree of magnification selected will determine the effective aperture, which varies between f/16 and f/32.

While its definition is slightly on the soft side, it's as good as most tele-converters will give, and the results should more than please you, especially considering the cost of the Quantaray. But be prepared for a certain amount of vignetting at the corners—it's inevitable and increases considerably should the prime lens be stopped down below f/4. Remember that, like the use of a telescope or other high-powered magnifying device, the Zoom Fotocular is subject to all the quirks of telephotography, so pick a clear day, use a fast lens and practice the other precautions we've already discussed for cutting through aerial haze when you use it.

Front lens devices and other attachments designed to magnify the image of your prime lens come and go with routine regularity, taking along a certain number of unwary buyers with them. Beyond the acquisition of either a Bushnell Spacemaster or the Ritz Zoom Fotocular, which represent opposite ends of the price spectrum, I would not recommend any of the other devices for telephotography—don't be lured into the idea that an optical miracle is just around the corner and that it can be had for a bargain price—it just isn't true. □

tele-converters

While the subject of tele-converters was covered in a chapter in *Interchangeable Lenses*, sufficient new developments have come about recently to merit another extensive look at them. For the benefit of those new to the interchangeable lens scene, let's first take a brief look at what a tele-converter is and how it works, before considering the pros and cons of one as a satisfactory substitute for additional telephoto lenses.

An inexpensive ($16-60) optical device containing a negative or Barlow lens, the tele-converter is an extension which fits between the camera body and lens to increase its focal length. Offered in two fixed powers or magnification ratios—2X and 3X—there is also a continuously variable or zoom model which spans the same ratios. Optically, the once-popular 1.5X converter is no longer adequate and should be avoided if you are offered one, no matter how good the price may be. All currently available converters are fitted with the necessary mechanical connecting linkage to retain the automatic diaphragm feature of a camera and lens when a converter is used.

The tele-converter will double (2X) or triple (3X) the effective focal length of any lens to which it is attached. Fit a 2X tele-converter to a standard 50mm lens and you have produced the equivalent of a 100mm lens; attach a 3X instead and the focal length becomes 150mm. At this point, it's not too difficult to see the potential of a pair of inexpensive converters and perhaps three prime lenses in forming a rather extensive focal length capability, without a tremendous

investment. Add a 2X and a 3X converter to a 50mm, a 135mm and a 300mm prime lens and you'd have access to nine focal lengths—50, 100, 135, 150, 270, 300, 405, 600 and 900mm—and at a fraction of the total cost if each of these focal lengths were a prime lens.

Equally attractive is the fact that even with a converter attached, your lens will still focus down to its minimum setting—your 50mm will become a 150mm with the ability to focus to 18-24 inches; your 135mm will turn into a 405mm but still focus to five feet; the 300 will be an ultraclose-focusing 900mm—now really, could you ask for anything more?

Ah hah, you say, there *must* be a hitch somewhere, and you're right, there are in fact *several* hitches. The first is an optical fact of life. As a converter doubles or triples the effective focal length of a prime lens without changing the size of the entrance pupil (width of the aperture), it also doubles/triples the effective aperture of the prime lens. Thus, a 2X converter used with a 50mm f/2 lens produces an *effective* focal length of 100mm but with an *effective* aperture of f/4—a two-stop reduction. The 3X converter used with the same lens produces a 150mm optic with an *effective* aperture of f/5.6.

But that's not all the bad news. The majority of prime lenses in this focal length require stopping down to about f/4 for optimum definition. As we'll see use of a converter demands the highest image quality possible from the prime lens, so the maximum aperture of

1-3. Two approaches to the new breed of highly corrected converters are represented by the Nikon TC-1 and TC-2 converters, and the Minolta 400mm f/5.6 MC APO Tele-Rokkor with MC 2X converter.

the combination necessary to produce optimum definition will be no greater than f/8 (2X) or f/11 (3X). With longer focal length prime lenses, this will introduce the requirement of a high shutter speed to reduce the image degradation of camera movement, and takes us to the use of a fast film—right where we'd be if we were using a slow-speed, long focal length prime lens. This 2-3 stop optical reduction in the maximum effective aperture, further compounded to 4-5 stops when we close the prime lens down for optimum performance, also results in a proportionately dimmer viewfinder image—making it far more difficult to focus and compose accurately under some lighting conditions.

Why is optimum performance of the prime lens so important? Because in effect the tele-converter magnifies or "spreads out" the center part of the image formed by the prime lens to cover the full negative format. If the prime lens to which the converter is attached is a high-quality optic, its image will be a good one; if the prime lens is mediocre in performance, the converter image will be poor. No tele-converter made can *improve* upon the performance of the prime lens; the very best it can do is retain the image quality of the prime lens. Thus, a good tele-converter will produce a good image from a good lens, and a poor image from a poor lens. A poor converter, however, will deliver a poor image from a good lens, and a wretched one from a poor lens.

In the process of magnifying the center of the image formed by the prime lens, the converter also magnifies any optical aberrations present in the prime lens. For this reason, the image-forming capability of any converter/prime lens combination can *never* equal that of the prime lens by itself and is in fact less, as the converter contains its own aberrations which are added to the final image. As converter magnification increases, the resulting optical performance of the combination has a tendency to decrease quite rapidly. For this reason, many users adhere to the old dictum that a fixed 2X converter is the maximum useful power if the best optical performance is desired.

Until recently, this situation was also complicated by market limitations. In the past, no major camera manufacturer saw fit to produce tele-converters, as they were more interested in selling prime lenses, not converters. So the converters were manufacturered by independent lens companies, who designed their product to work with *all* lenses, not with a specific focal length or optical design. This meant that the optical design of any tele-converter was a compromise at best, and it was not unusual to find that one brand which gave good results with a particular lens did not perform as well with other optics of the same focal length. So if you bought the same brand of tele-converter as your neighbor and got better (or worse) results than he did, here's the probable answer—providing that all other variables remained the same. But this situation is now changing, as we'll see in a moment.

At this point, let's summarize and look at the positive side for a moment. With a converter, we have the capability to double/triple the effective focal length of any lens, providing that we're willing to trade 2-3 lens openings and accept the reduced lens speed and darker viewfinder image. In addition, we must also sacrifice approximately two more f-stops for the best possible image quality from the combination. But as most converters only weigh about four ounces, we now have a lightweight telephoto which is 2-3 times more powerful than the prime lens without the converter. This can be a big advantage in many cases—one major lens manufacturer's 300mm weighs two pounds, eight ounces. With a converter added, it becomes a 900mm weighing three pounds, or some eight pounds, 13 ounces less than the same manufacturer's comparable 800mm.

We also now have a 900mm that will focus down to 13 feet, while the comparable 800mm mentioned will focus only to 60 feet! How is it possible that a tele-converter does *not* change the minimum focusing distance of the prime lens when used with it? Simple—using the converter changes the method by which the lens achieves its focus. Prime lenses usually focus by shifting the entire lens forward in relation to the focal plane. But as the converter always remains fixed between the camera body and prime lens, focusing when the

telephoto photography/63

combination is used results in only the prime lens shifting. In effect, focusing is now achieved by reducing the actual focal length of the combination. The result is similar to that of the close-focusing zoom lenses which use front element focusing, and offers some interesting possibilities for "macro" work, as we'll see.

And what happens to depth of field when a tele-converter is introduced into the optical system? The converter/prime lens combination provides a depth of field equal to that of a prime telephoto lens of equivalent focal length. Thus our 300mm f/5.6 lens converts to a 600mm f/11 with a depth of field which is the same as a 600mm prime lens stopped down to f/11. In essence, this means that your 300mm and 2X converter will produce the same degree of space compression with the accompanying shallow depth that a 600mm prime lens would. Because of this, you are subject to the same requirement for accurate focusing and do not lose the creative potential of a long focal length prime lens when you use a converter/prime lens combination instead.

As tele-converters are available in a wide price range and under a variety of brand names, I'm sure you want to know what you can expect in the way of performance, and if the more expensive ones are really worth the extra money asked. While there are some recent exceptions to the following evaluation which we'll consider at length later on, all converters, regardless of brand name, will show definition slightly on the soft side, with a resultant lowering of contrast. Both definition and contrast will be better in the center of the picture than at the edges, and both will increase to some degree as you stop the prime lens down, but don't expect the increase to be a dramatic one. On the average, you should expect to lose between 25 and 50 percent of the prime lens's sharpness in the center of

the picture, and up to 60-80 percent at the edges. Discouraging? Yes and no, depending upon what uses you have in mind for a tele-converter.

Exhaustive tests have turned up a few interesting facts about the use of tele-converters which may help you to make up your own mind whether or not one will be of use to you. Almost without exception, they appear to work best with prime lens focal lengths from 50mm to 105mm at close distances, and with focal lengths 400mm and above at long range. They are not suitable for use with most zoom lenses, as the optical balance of a zoom is finely honed to begin with, and most converter/zoom combinations I've tried literally destroy this balance, resulting in some horrible examples of how bad a

1. 50mm lens at infinity—no converter. The remainder of this sequence demonstrates the effect of a converter on moderate length telephotos.
2. 50mm lens at infinity—2X converter.
3. 85mm lens at infinity—no converter.
4. 85mm lens at infinity—2X converter.
5. 105mm lens at infinity—no converter.
6. 105mm lens at infinity—2X converter.
7. 135mm lens at infinity—2X converter.

converter can really be. This gives you two rather distinct uses for a converter which will produce the most acceptable results, and one which you should avoid.

Coupled to a 50-105mm, the converter can be used for portrait work; the results will be slightly on the soft side but that need not be considered a total disadvantage in this type of work—and many would even view it as an advantage. Used with the 500mm or longer focal lengths, a converter only deals with a small number of light rays gathered at a narrow angle and so its best optical area, the center, is in control. This will produce reasonable pictorial results in many cases, although the edges will still be noticeably soft. But many such subjects do not require high definition or contrast. A tele-converter is more than adequate when it comes to dealing with such subjects as the red blob of sun setting behind a landscape.

How sharp is sharp? It's a well-known fact that some people can accept a greater loss of image quality than others and still be content with the results. Since a loss of sharpness is often acceptable to many, and there is no standard of comparison by which to judge, this acceptance factor is something that no one but you can determine. And if you've never owned a long focal length prime lens before, will you even know what you're missing? It is safe to say however, that those who work primarily with color slides and giant enlargements are not likely to be as satisfied as the others who work primarily in black-and-white, restricting their final print size to 8x10, or those who settle for wallet-size color prints.

There's another side to the use of a tele-converter that should be explored briefly. As the converter does not alter the minimum focusing distance of the prime lens with which it is used, a 50mm lens and 2X converter will produce a 100mm equivalent which focuses down to 18 inches, a distance comparable to that of a so-called 100mm "macro" lens, but with one big difference. As the converter/prime lens combination focuses by shortening the actual focal length of the two for closer distances, the apparent perspective produced at magnification ratios approaching 1:1 is closer to that of a 75mm prime lens.

Because the converter demands a comparatively short extension of the prime lens to alter its focus, the two-stop reduction in the effective aperture of the combination focused at infinity becomes closer to a single f-stop reduction when used for close-up work in the 1:2 magnification ratio range. How can you achieve such magnification ratios? You can do so by installing a short extension tube *between* the converter and prime lens. This placement is very important, as the converter has been designed to work at a fixed distance from the film plane. While the results will not match those obtainable with one of the lenses to be discussed in the following chapter, they will be more than adequate with three-dimensional subjects such as bees, butterflies and flowers, where good definition is necessary only in the center of the frame and the softness of the less critical edges can work to focus viewer attention on the subject. Thus, those on a limited lens budget who put a converter to use in this manner can also enjoy some

4

5

6

7

of the benefits of a "macro" telephoto without having to invest in one immediately.

As a result of having read this far, you may believe that the converter situation is bleak, but let me inject one positive note of optimism—I've received a good deal of mail from readers indicating that they are satisfied with the results obtained with their converters—and none from the other side of the question. As I see it, this correlates with my earlier statement that mating a converter to one brand and focal length lens may work very well, while with other combinations, it may not work at all. It also correlates with an individual's ability to visually tolerate a certain amount of unsharpness without being disturbed. But one inescapable fact remains: There are many who are satisfied with the occasional use of a tele-converter.

Personally, I would not suggest that you buy one as a substitute for expanding your accessory lens capability with other prime lenses, but rather as a temporary expedient which will permit you to enjoy telephotography until your budget allows you to purchase other prime optics. Those who have specialized telephoto interests such as nature photography will do well to stay with the use of a prime lens, but for others who will seldom use the reach of a 400mm or longer lens, or who wish to experiment with ultra close-ups of three-dimensional subjects, the tele-converter can provide a low-cost means of bridging that gap whenever an unexpected picture opportunity comes their way. The question really boils down to the traditional argument that has revolved around the use of tele-converters since they first became available—is it better to depend upon one, with all its attendant faults and disadvantages, or to come away with no picture?

What are the recent developments in converters which I mentioned earlier? The advance most applicable to those converters presently manufactured by independent lens houses has been multicoating. Early converters were coated, of course, and worked as well as could be expected with coated lenses. But with the advent of multicoating on prime optics, it was to be expected that such would be extended to both filters and converters.

In the case of converters, it's certainly desirable that the converter used with a multicoated prime lens also be multicoated, in order to reduce possible flare and

66/telephoto photography

prevent ghosting from degrading the image quality beyond the degree of loss normally expected from converter use. Since color photography is much more universal today than it was some years ago, it's also important that the multicoating have as close to a neutral color transmission as possible to prevent it from interfering with any color bias of the prime lens. As some prime lenses have a warm bias and others a cold bias, the last thing you want is a prime lens with one bias and a converter with an opposite bias.

While multicoating has been no major breakthrough insofar as converter design is concerned, it has at least allowed the lowly negative lens to keep pace with the state-of-the-art in prime lens technology. But, should you replace your present converter with one that's multicoated? *I* really can't say—are *you* satisfied with the results? If you're using multicoated prime lenses and your converter doesn't seem to deliver results as good as it did with the single-coated optics, you might try one of the multicoated variety just to see what difference it might make.

Replacing an older converter with a new one can have a significant effect on your pictures—if your present converter is either a 1.5X power, or a 2X-3X more than five years old. Although no really outstanding optical design changes have taken place in that period, there have been considerable refinements which make today's tele-converter a far better

1. 50mm lens at infinity—no converter. The remainder of this sequence demonstrates the effect of a converter when used with long telephotos. (Sequence by Ron Berkenblitt.)
2. 200mm lens at infinity—no converter.
3. 200mm lens at infinity—2X converter.
4. 300mm lens at infinity—no converter.
5. 300mm lens at infinity—2X converter.
6. 400mm lens at infinity—no converter.
7. 400mm lens at infinity—2X converter.

buy than those of 5-10 years ago. While the 1.5X design was never really competent, the day of the two- or three-element converter is also definitely passé.

At least two Japanese optical houses now offer six- or seven-element converters, one brand of which is currently imported to this country. These provide worthwhile alternatives to the more common four-element design primarily in one respect—the use of the extra elements permits a better image correction when the prime lens is used at its maximum aperture, and somewhat better edge sharpness at most apertures.

While far more important to the future of the tele-converter, the other developments of interest are o far less likely to obsolete the converter we presently use due to the cost involved. But at the same time, the development by major camera manufacturers of converters specifically computed for use with their own lens's formulas holds considerable promise for the future.

Earlier, I mentioned the trend toward compact cameras and lenses, pointing out specific examples through the moderate telephoto range. To that point, it's technologically possible to significantly reduce the size of current optics, while improving their optical qualities at the same time. But what about the longer telephoto designs—how can they be reduced in size and weight?

Use of the tele-converter as one possible answer is currently being explored at this writing by Canon, Minolta and Nikon. Canon started the ball rolling back in 1973 with the announcement of its 300mm f/2.8 fluorite lens, complete with its own 2X converter specifically computed for use with that lens. Minolta followed recently with its own 400mm f/5.6 and 600mm f/6.3 APO telephotos (which also utilize a fluorite element), supplied with a specially formulated 2X converter which incorporates five optical elements in three groups. While all of these converters are designed for optimum performance as an integral part of the optical system of the lens with which they are supplied, they are also usable with other lenses in the manufacturer's line, although performance may not be quite as satisfactory.

Granted, each of these optics is expensive at this time, but they are also compact, fast, high-performance lenses. Speculate a few years ahead when high-quality telephotos equipped with a converter specifically designed for their use are available in a variety of focal lengths—you'll be able to own and carry half the number of lenses presently required to cover a given focal length range. The current optics are smaller

telephoto photography/67

but somewhat heavier than other lenses of comparable focal lengths, yet with their converter attached, they weigh less than half of that equivalent focal length.

Nikon has taken a somewhat different direction, but its 2X TC-1 and TC-2 converters, first used at the 1976 summer Olympics by press photographers at the invitation of Nikon, are no less a milestone in converter design. Manufactured for use with all Nikon lenses (the TC-1 with 200mm or shorter and the 500mm Reflex Nikkor; the TC-2 with 300mm or greater and the 105mm Micro Nikkor), these converters produce no detectable image deterioration, contrast loss or flare at any aperture, and probably represent the ultimate in converter quality which has been achieved at this time.

1. 500mm lens at infinity—no converter.
2. 500mm lens at infinity—2X converter.
3. 1000mm lens at infinity—no converter.
4. 1000mm lens at infinity—2X converter.

With its new five-element converter presently under development, Soligor strikes off in yet another direction. In terms of image magnification, this one has every other competitor on the market beat—it's a 4X tele-converter. While its use results in an effective aperture four stops smaller than that to which the prime lens is set (f/5.6 becomes f/22), it does deliver a full 400 percent magnification, or to put it another way, you can fill the negative with one-quarter of the image seen by the prime lens.

We've looked at three new approaches to converter design and function, and with these developments already announced and in production, you can well imagine that other manufacturers have other concepts in the works. While these (as well as the new ones to come) are not inexpensive, they do signal the dawning of a new era in tele-converters—one in which you will not have to settle for optical transmission much less than that of which the prime lens alone is capable, as long as you're willing to pay the price.

This means that the tele-converter market will expand into two segments—the expensive, near-perfect converters just described, and the less expensive, less perfect ones with which we're presently acquainted. There should be some optical "fallout" from the former which can improve the latter without a significant increase in cost to the consumer. Why, the next thing you know, somebody will come up with a practical tele-converter concept which produces the desired focal length with little or no loss in lens speed—and it's the possibility of such revolutionary optics that makes the next decade of lens design certain to be twice as exciting as the last one! □

telephoto photography/69

macro-focusing telephotos

The most recent trend in macro lens design (other than the close-focusing zooms) has been the introduction of a variety of 90-105mm optics which are designed to focus down to approximately 18 inches—a distance at which they will provide a 1:2 reproduction ratio. Like the close-focusing zooms discussed at length in another section of this book, most of the macro telephotos do not give you the capability of true macro photography—images larger than 1:1.

In this respect, they are essentially moderate telephoto lenses in which the close-focusing range has been extended to that of a normal focal length. Like the normal focal length macro lenses, this is done by lengthening the helical focusing mechanism in the lens barrel to achieve a greater amount of separation between the film plane and optical center of the lens. Also like the normal macro focal length, they will deliver only a 1:2 reproduction ratio by themselves. To achieve the 1:1 ratio, it is necessary to install an accessory intermediate tube between the camera body and lens.

While it is more accurate to consider these lenses as close-focusing telephotos rather than true macro lenses, there are two significant differences between the macro telephoto and the so-called "macro" zoom: The macro telephotos uniformly provide the 1:2 reproduction ratio, which most such zooms do not, and they are optically corrected to deliver their maximum performance in the close-focusing range. Unlike those close-focusing zooms which claim macro capability, the macro telephotos do possess a flat field and have little or no linear distortion, making them far more suitable for copying flat subjects such as documents, stamps, etc.

Current macro telephotos range between 90mm and 105mm in focal length, with a maximum aperture of either f/2.5-f/2.8 or f/3.5-f/4 and a minimum aperture of f/22 or f/32, depending upon their particular design. Like regular telephotos of comparable focal length, their optical construction is quite simple, usually five elements in three or four groups. An exception to this general rule is the 90mm Vivitar Macro Series 1, which incorporates an additional three elements in its 1:1 adapter tube, or "macro corrector-lens adapter," as Vivitar calls it. When the macro corrector-lens adapter is used, the main elements in the lens move away from those in the adapter during focusing. This concept is borrowed from astronomical optics to compensate for aberrations which are produced when the lens is moved away from the film plane during photography in the 1:2 to 1:1 reproduction ratio range.

All macro telephotos are fitted with automatic diaphragms and are compatible with open-aperture metering. Like the 50-55mm macro lenses, the front element of most macro telephotos is deeply recessed in the lens barrel, making the use of a lens shade academic. Those designs in which the front element is close to the end of the barrel should be used with a shade whenever the possibility of flare exists, as this can be a very critical element in close-up work.

Why use a close-focusing telephoto lens? Although the 50-55mm macro lenses do very well for flat copy work, they are often at a disadvantage when dealing with three-dimensional objects. If you're working with living subjects, such as insects, the normal macro requires that you move in very close to the subject to achieve a suitable image size. This can pose problems in terms of lighting, as you and the camera may well interfere with the source of illumination striking the subject.

It can also make things difficult if the subject happens to be a flighty creature who doesn't particularly enjoy having a huge piece of shiny glass shoved within inches of him. And coming as close to the subject as you must can also cause apparent perspective distortion, with objects close to the camera appearing to be much larger than other more distant ones. The macro telephoto solves these and other such problems by allowing you to

One prime advantage of a macro telephoto is shown here—it keeps you at a sufficient distance from your subject to avoid interfering with lighting while shooting at a 1:1 ratio.

work at distances more than double that of the normal macro lens, while achieving the same image size.

Considering the pros and cons, the primary value of a macro telephoto over the more traditional close-up tools, such as an extension bellows, extension tubes, and positive diopter lenses is simply that of portability and ease of operation, assuming that the lens used in each of the other cases is of equivalent quality. But carrying an extension bellows into the field or juggling a set of extension tubes is not the fastest, surest way to work, especially with living subjects. Yet when you combine some of their qualities with the lens in the form of the longer helical focusing tube, you make close-up photography in the field a comparative breeze.

Readers interested in reaching into the true macro range will be more inclined to use one of the short-mount or bellows macro lenses. These are essentially a macro-corrected lens but without the focusing tube or automatic diaphragm feature, and were once quite popular in the 50-55mm focal length until the introduction and acceptance of the macro optic with its own focusing capability caused interest in them to decline. But as we know, everything seems to travel in circles, and so the recent announcement by Honeywell, Konica and Minolta of 100-105mm bellows lenses to fit the Pentax K, Konica and Minolta cameras signals a renewal of interest in working with bellows-mount macro lenses on the part of many photographers. Past

telephoto photography/71

experience has also shown that no major camera manufacturer brings forth a new lens without some strong indication that it is wanted by photographers, and when three such companies enter the field, you can be sure that more such lenses are on the way.

This resurgence of interest in the bellows-mount macro telephoto has been accompanied by provision for automatic diaphragm operation through the use of newer bellows units which provide mechanical coupling linkage from the lens to the camera. As exposure metering through the lens is usually accomplished with the lens stopped down to its shooting aperture, there is no need for manual calculation of exposure with such optics, as in the past. In essence, the use of the short-mount macro lens with an extension bellows has been made easier and faster, which no doubt helps to account for its new-found popularity in moderate telephoto lengths.

To determine how large an image size you can obtain with a given bellows and the 100-105mm macro lens designed for use with it, you must know the maximum extension of which the bellows is capable. As the degree of magnification is limited by the bellows extension and the focal length of the lens used, it is obtained by dividing the maximum bellows extension by the focal length of the lens. For example, suppose that your bellows will extend four inches or 200mm. If you use a 50mm bellows-mount lens, the maximum magnification will be 4X or 4:1—four times life-size. Now switch to a 100mm lens on the same bellows and your maximum magnification becomes 2X or 2:1—twice life-size; the longer the focal length, the less the degree of magnification that can be obtained. If greater magnification ratios are required, it is possible to mount extension tubes between the camera body and the bellows, but this rapidly becomes cumbersome, and its value will depend to a large extent upon the quality of the lens and your ability to release the shutter at a very slow speed without inducing camera movement.

From a theoretical point of view, the performance of a macro lens is supposedly less satisfactory when used at distances beyond a 1:10 ratio than that of a comparable nonmacro focal length used at the same point of focus. If we are to accept that on faith, it then becomes very difficult for many readers to justify the purchase of a macro lens—normal or telephoto—and especially those who are fascinated by the possibilities, but who also realistically accept that their use for such a special purpose lens would be quite limited.

While the statement above *is* true in theory, I'm happy to point out to you that optical theory does not always apply to practical usage. If you find it difficult to spend the money for a macro telephoto because of the limited use you expect to have for it, consider purchasing one *instead* of a nonmacro 90-105mm telephoto. Just as many photographers have substituted the 50-55mm macro for their camera's normal lens in everyday shooting and are pleased with the results, so can the macro telephoto be substituted for its nonmacro equivalent. You'll find it very difficult to distinguish any difference in performance between the two.

As the macro telephotos are as fast as most of the nonmacro equivalents and utilize the same automatic diaphragm feature, the major disadvantage of such a substitution becomes that of overall weight and a slight increase in size caused by the extended design of the lens barrel. But in return for living with a few extra ounces and possibly an extra inch or two in length, you'll have a moderate telephoto which will do double-duty and do it admirably.

Just for fun, let's suppose for a moment that you already own both a 50-55mm macro lens and a 100-105mm telephoto—not an uncommon combination

1-2. The 105mm Micro-Nikkor with PN-1 ring and the Pentax Bellows 100mm represent two different approaches to macro telephotos. The Nikkor can be used as a normal lens, but since the Pentax has no focusing ring of its own, it must be used with a bellows attachment.

3-4. The intricate works of a tiny music box movement are reproduced at a 1:1 ratio (3). Add a 2X converter to the macro telephoto and a 2:1 ratio is possible, as in this glimpse inside a solid-state watch (4). Sharpness does not suffer in an 8x10 enlargement from the converter/macro telephoto combination.

telephoto photography/73

1

2

74/telephoto photography

in many gadget bags these days. Under such circumstances, a 90-105mm macro telephoto would obviously not be the most useful way to invest your money, yet there are occasions when you'd like the benefit of one. So what to do? There's one answer of which you may not have thought yet—add a tele-converter to your 50-55mm macro!

Before you start tossing back all the limitations of a converter that were outlined in the previous chapter, think of the solution in a positive way. A 2X converter of good quality will double the focal length to 100-110mm, reduce the f/3.5 aperture of your macro lens to an effective aperture of approximately f/6.3, retain the 8-10-inch close-focusing distance of your lens and provide the depth of field and apparent perspective of the macro telephoto. As you would probably stop your 50-55mm macro down to at least f/5.6 for use, the combination becomes an f/11 optic—still highly useful under most macro lighting conditions.

Because you'll use the 100-110mm effective focal length primarily with three-dimensional subjects such as flowers, insects or tabletop objects, you're primarily interested in the center of the frame and so the slight softness encountered at the edges of the picture area should not prove visually disturbing. And any flat copy work which you may have can be done with the 50-55mm macro, as in the past.

Once you've considered the possibility in that light, let me suggest that you fit a good converter to your macro and shoot a few test shots to prove that I'm not talking though my hat. I'm certain that you'll agree that this is not really a bad solution after all—you get most of the benefits of a macro telephoto lens for the price of a tele-converter,

which can give your budget a healthy lift instead of taxing it to the limit. □

1-4. Most normal 50mm camera lenses focus to 18 inches, reproducing my one-inch pet plastic fly as shown (1). Changing to a 105mm macro telephoto without using the 1:1 tube gives a magnification ratio of 1:2, as shown in (2). Adding the 1:1 tube to the 105mm macro produces (3), while adding a 2X converter to the same combination produces (4). Note the softened contrast in (4) that results from the use of a converter in this instance.

tripods

What're your most important criteria for selecting a tripod? If you're like many amateurs, the chances are good that you'll consider cost, size and weight—in that order. While unfortunate, it's also true—most tripods are sold by those three factors. Buying the least expensive, smallest and lightest tripod possible is self-defeating, yet if you stand in camera shops for a week as I have, you'd be amazed at just how many of the three-legged monsters are bought by customers (or sold by camera salesmen) who believe that if it's small and light enough to be carried, it shouldn't be very expensive, and so why pay more than absolutely necessary for something that you'll probably use very little anyway?

Strangely enough, customers are not unwilling to spend $1000 or more for a camera outfit without blinking an eyelash, but begrudge the price of a suitable tripod, trying to keep their outlay for one below $30, if at all possible. Should you already own a tripod and have since acquired an interest in telephotography, the chances are excellent that the one you presently have is not suitable for use with a long lens. If you're not willing or able to replace it with one that is, don't cop out and try to blame the poor quality of your pictures on your telephoto lens.

As we close our discussion on the ins-and-outs of telephoto photography, I would hope that you have at least resigned yourself to the use of a tripod on *many* occasions, even if you're not too happy about the prospects of working with one. I know of very few photographers who actually enjoy lugging a tripod around, setting it up for use and then dismantling the setup after they've tripped the shutter. While I'm the first to agree with you that a tripod is a burden under most circumstances, I hope you'll agree with me when I proclaim it as a necessary evil for much of the type of work we've been discussing.

A tripod isn't the only form of camera support that can be used to do the job, but it *is* the best, if properly chosen. While gunstocks, monopods and shoulder pods all have their place in telephotography, a tripod is by far the best possible insurance against camera movement. Because of the average amateur's great reluctance to buy a tripod in the first place, and to buy the right one when he/she does settle on the idea, a few hints are in order to help you make the correct selection the first time around.

If money were of no object, buying the steadiest, sturdiest tripod would pose no problems. But the steadiest, sturdiest tripod is not always the one best suited for your needs. Certainly, you wouldn't carry a 100-pound wooden tripod on your back as did the old-time photographers trekking through the wilderness, nor would you outfit yourself with a mule to carry the tripod and your equipment. So a certain amount of compromise is necessary when it comes to the selection of a tripod. The trick is to find the unit which involves the least amount of compromise while doing an adequate job efficiently.

While portability is a prime requisite of any tripod, this is

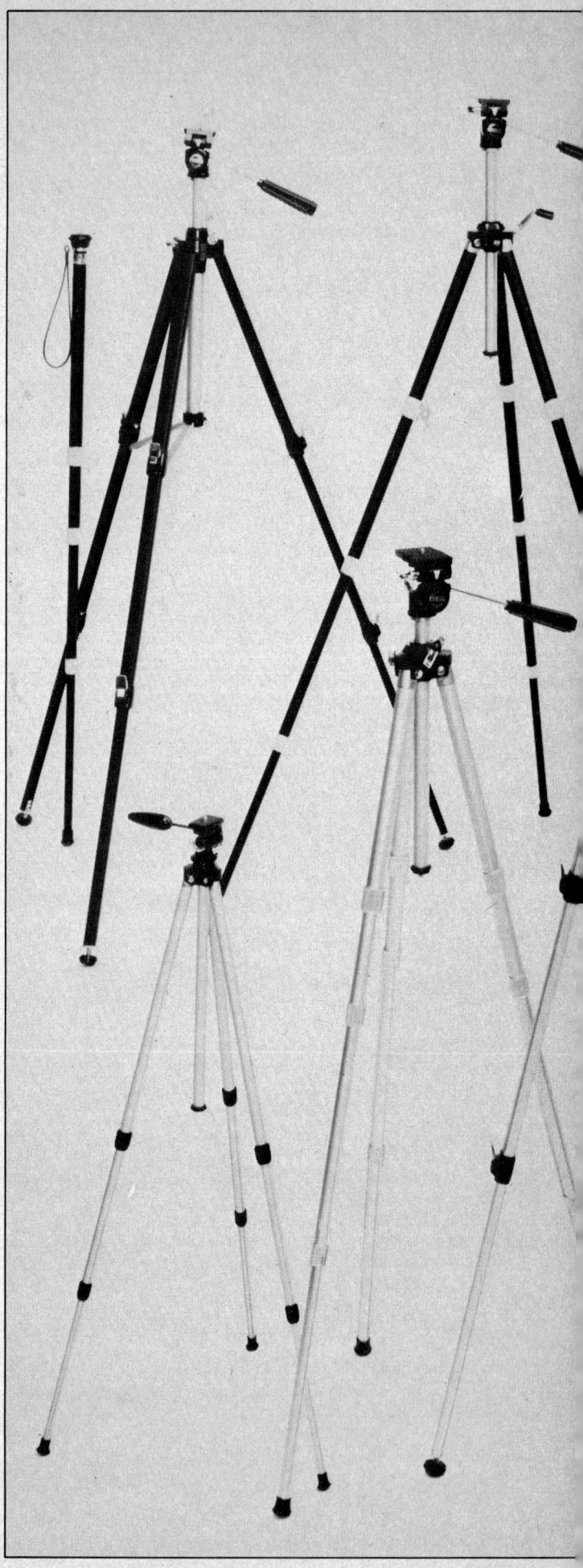

Tripods galore! Soligor offers an even dozen—one of the many lines on the market. Whichever brand you buy, choose your tripod with care, as it must be able to support your camera and telephoto lens without vibration.

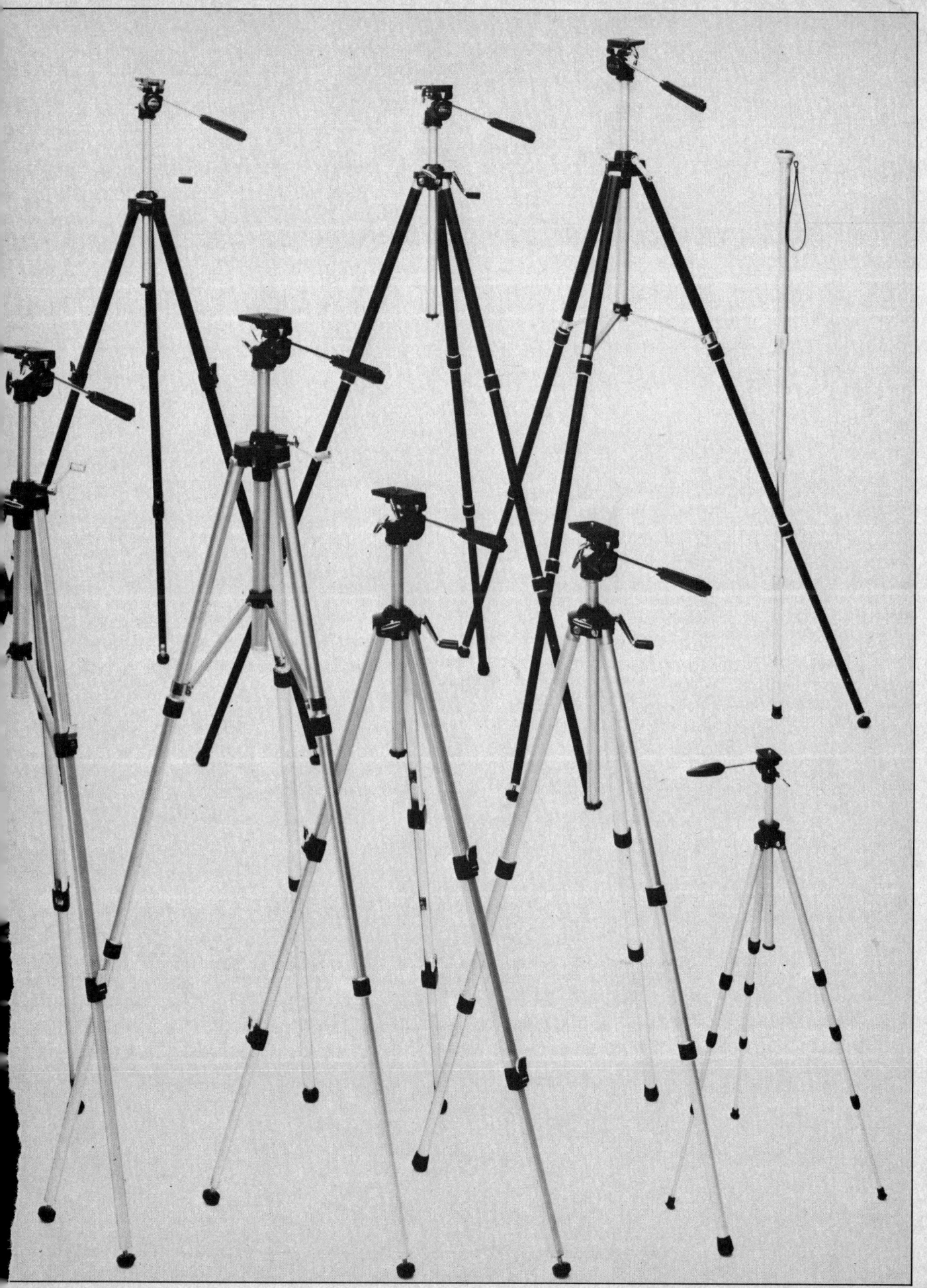

telephoto photography/77

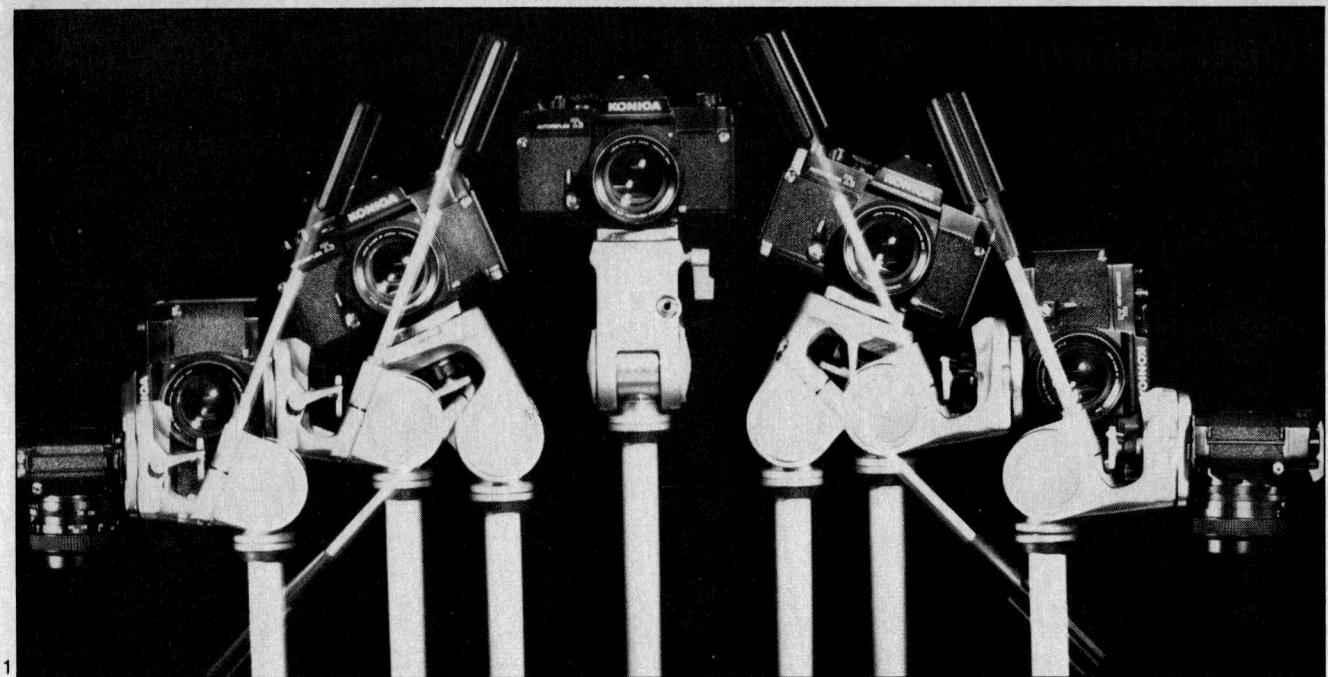

the first sales feature which should be compromised on your part. Those nine-sectioned legs which extend to form a 60-inch tripod are dandy for carrying, but are so insubstantial once they're extended that they invite shake from the nearest passing breeze. Ideally, the extended tripod must be absolutely rigid, with no tendency to waver or buckle when weight is applied to its top. Whether of U-channel or tubular construction, a two-section tripod is the best, a three-section one probably the best all-around compromise, and a four-section unit usable only if you absolutely need the added 5-6 inches of height to meet our next requirement. If you decide upon a three- or four-section unit, consider the advantages of center pole leg braces.

Those geared-center-column arrangements are also useful for making quick vertical adjustments, but the tripod should be tall enough by itself when the legs are fully extended to be used without having to crank up the column. Balancing a camera and heavy lens atop that solitary pole extended another 6-9 inches above the tripod only defeats the purpose of having three solid legs to begin with.

Although just as important as selecting a tripod of sufficient height and sturdy design, the choice of pan head is equally overlooked by the enthusiast. As most inexpensive tripods come equipped with an inexpensive head, the amateur buys one and gets the other without bothering to consider that the two units are separate entities although they are used together. For openers, those old-fashioned ball-and-socket heads are not only outdated,

1. A good tripod panhead will permit quick camera orientation, as demonstrated by the Duo-Pan action of a Slik Master tripod.
2. The monopod, or single-tripod leg, is a sometime substitute for the more bulky tripod, but its use still requires a steady hand with long lenses.
3. A good, solid tripod is still your best insurance with 400mm and longer optics.
4. With very heavy or long lenses, or when the wind is blowing even slightly, it's a good idea to use two tripods, one attached to the camera body and the other to the tripod block on the lens.

but most are strained to their capacity to reliably hold a moderately heavy camera and lens.

The camera platform of a good, solid pan head should be sufficient in size to hold the largest camera you expect to use with it. It should revolve (pan) smoothly, tilt easily and lock securely in whatever position you decide upon. While some heads use a single lever for both functions, those equipped with separate controls seem easier for many photographers to use efficiently. The platform slotting should be sufficient to provide for balanced mounting of the camera body, its tripod attaching screw should be of adequate length to seat completely into the camera's tripod socket, and the wedging screw used to lock the attaching screw should be large enough to operate easily and securely.

Much has been made recently of quick-release features on some pan heads, and a variety of such adapters have been placed on the market by accessory manufacturers. These usually work by attaching one portion of the release mechanism to the pan head and the other to the camera's tripod socket. Slip the two pieces together and flip a switch, turn a locking nut or slide a clamping device into place and the camera is supposedly secured to the tripod; reverse the procedure and

you can separate them instantly.

Do you need the quick-release feature? Probably not. Most that I've seen which are reliable require almost as much time and effort to activate as you'd spend releasing the wedging screw and spinning the attaching screw from the tripod socket. While it's an open invitation to manufacturers of such devices to take me to task, I'd suggest that you forego the use of a quick-release mechanism when using long focal length lenses, as it just introduces another weak link in what is really a tenuous chain to begin with. Besides, the ones I've seen which are really firm and solid in use have not proven that handy for me to operate.

Incidentally, I've seen numerous photographers over the years who fold up their tripod, leaving the camera and lens attached, tuck it under their arm and head off for another location. This is especially dangerous when you've got a long, heavy lens attached, as cameras have actually been known to fall off on occasion. A potentially greater danger comes from carrying your equipment in this manner—one stumble and you may do in an expensive camera, lens *and* tripod. If you have to reposition the tripod a distance from where you've

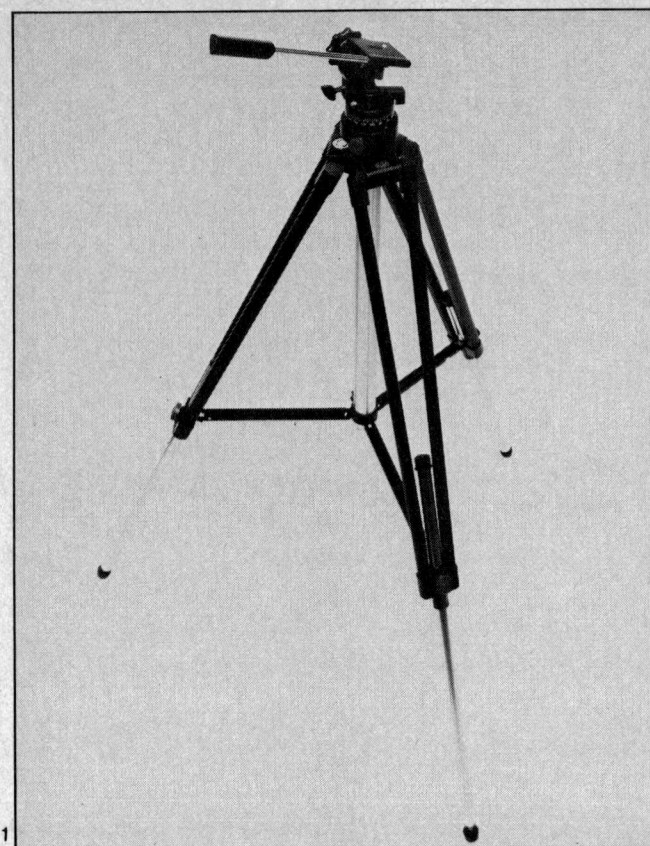

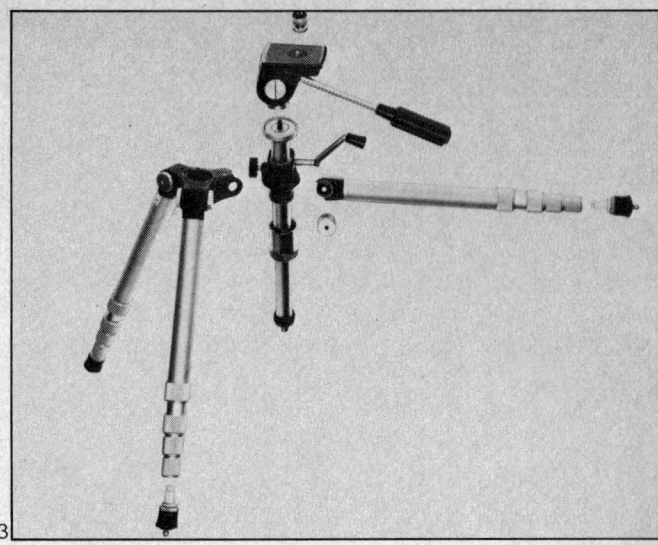

been working, the use of a tripod dolly is highly recommended whenever feasible. When the use of such is not possible because of terrain or other physical problems, dismount the camera and lens, carrying it separately from the tripod.

Don't overlook potential uses for your tripod other than telephotography when you're shopping around. Some permit leg adjustment to use the tripod almost at ground level, and others allow the pan head to be removed and mounted to the bottom of the center column for low-angle, close-up or copy work. But whenever you consider a tripod with such special features, make certain that use of the feature(s) in question does not introduce instability.

If space permitted, I could continue discussing the selection of a proper tripod beyond your endurance to read, believe it or not. But I think that you've gotten the idea at which I'm driving—an inexpensive tripod is less than satisfactory for telephotography, and in order to acquire one that is suitable, you must be willing to spend a little extra money and shop the various brands to find one that operates smoothly and efficiently while providing as solid a mount for your camera/lens as possible.

Since there are literally dozens and dozens of tripods available these days, with more arriving on the market every month, a thorough examination of the various models can really cloud the issue if you're not firmly committed to the basic essentials. Don't let the addition of novelties such as quick-release devices, spirit level, pan head markings for panoramic photography, etc. sway you from your real purpose—locating a solid, sturdy and functional tripod. The ones used to illustrate this final chapter of our discussion are representative of the features found in the vast numbers and varieties available at this writing, and their appearance here is not to be misconstrued as the author's personal favorites or recommended models—I'm still lugging that 100-pound monstrosity around! ☐

1. For those who want a rock-solid tripod for use with large-format cameras, the twin-strut leg design of tripods like the Bilora 3142 provides the greatest rigidity.
2. Whether channel or tubular in construction, the leg extensions should lock securely and unlock easily.
3. The latest wrinkle in tripod design is shown in the Slik System tripod—the modular concept permits the user to modify his tripod for specific applications.
4. Tripods like the Prinz Samson which feature a reversible center column are useful for copy or close-up work.